LANGUAGE AND STYLE SERIES
General Editor: Stephen Ullmann
XII

SYNONYMY
AND
LINGUISTIC ANALYSIS

ROY HARRIS

OXFORD
BASIL BLACKWELL
MCMLXXIII

o 631 14030 1

Library of Congress Catalog Card No.

73—169532

PRINTED IN GREAT BRITAIN
BY A. T. BROOME AND SON, 18 ST. CLEMENT'S, OXFORD
AND BOUND BY THE KEMP HALL BINDERY, OXFORD

Contents

Introduction

One way in which we may seek to improve our understanding of the nature of language is to consider what follows from adopting particular procedures and devices as permissible in descriptive linguistic analysis. The present study examines the theoretical consequences of supposing that a correct linguistic analysis of a natural language may, in certain cases, treat as identical in meaning two sentences—or, more generally, two items of whatever grammatical status (*expressions* will serve here as a neutral term)—not identical in form. This supposition may be called for convenience the *synonymy postulate*, and any pair of expressions related in the appropriate way may be said to be *synonymous* in the language in question.

Terminologically, the above proposals involve an extension of the traditional usage, which restricts the term *synonym* and its cognates to expressions of the kind which appear as lemmata in conventional dictionaries (chiefly common nouns, verbs, adjectives and adverbs). That usage goes back to the definition given in Aristotle's *Rhetoric* III, 2, 1404 b, and was continued by the eighteenth- and nineteenth-century synonymists who compiled synonym dictionaries of the modern European languages. But it has been superseded by a broader usage which sanctions speaking of synonymy 'not only in the case of single words, but both above and below words'.[1] In current discussions of the subject, words, bound morphs, phrases, clauses, sentences and sequences of sentences may be cited as examples of synonymous expressions. The broader usage does not require us to commit ourselves in advance as to the exact grammatical status of the expressions under discussion.

By adopting the synonymy postulate, we make available for use in descriptive linguistic analysis a particular kind of statement, which it is here proposed to call a *synonymity statement*. Synonymity statements may be characterized as statements cast in or reducible to the form

'*a* and *b* are synonymous in *L*'

or 	'*a* and *b* are not synonymous in *L*'

---

[1] Collinson, 1939.

where L is the particular language under description, and a and b are expressions of that language. Such statements present a comparison of certain linguistic items in respect of their linguistic meanings, abstracting from the meanings in question and giving simply an assessment of 'semantic sameness' vs. 'semantic difference'. They thus formulate what are called *synonymity hypotheses* in the terminology suggested by Naess.[1] The status of the hypotheses is comparable to that of hypotheses in other empirical sciences: they 'may be said to make claims about actual or possible interpretative processes in the same way as hypotheses about certain substances being explosives make claims about actual or possible explosions.'[2] (A hypothesis of this kind may, of course, be involved in certain explanations without being overtly formulated: it would then be necessary, strictly, to speak of the use of a 'synonymity hypothesis' rather than the use of a 'synonymity statement', but for present purposes the distinction is of no consequence.)

The availability of synonymity statements opens up certain possibilities—but also raises certain problems—in descriptive phonology, grammar and semantics, and these issues will provide the focal points of discussion throughout the following chapters. But it may be as well to point out here that there are many 'questions of synonymy' which do not fall within the scope of the present inquiry.

We shall not be interested, for example, in claims that may be made by native speakers to the effect that certain expressions they use 'have the same meaning'. 'As a native speaker of English,' asserts a recent writer, 'I know that "oculist" is exactly synonymous with "eye doctor".'[3] Now it may or may not be the case that such a claim coincides with the description of *oculist* and *eye-doctor* in a systematic semantic analysis of English. But if we are interested in the 'correctness' of the claim in this sense, it makes little difference whether it is advanced by a native speaker of English or a Martian. A different matter would be to discover what any native speaker thinks he is claiming when he claims that one expression is 'exactly synonymous' with another. But that too would be of merely subsidiary interest, for present purposes, to the elucidation of what a linguist would be explaining by postulating the synonymity of *oculist* and *eye-doctor* as part of the linguistic knowledge of speakers of English.

Similarly, such matters as proposals concerning distributional criteria for synonymity, or the 'quantification' of synonymy, are of no

[1] Naess 1953.   [2] Naess 1953, p. 17.   [3] Searle 1969, p. 11.

interest here. In connexion with the former, Chomsky observes that 'many linguists have proposed that synonymy be somehow measured in terms of degree of distributional similarity (cf. e.g. H. M. Honigswald *Language Change and Linguistic Reconstruction*, Chicago, 1960; H. Frei 'Désaccords' *Cahiers Ferdinand de Saussure* 18.35-51, 1961) and have then concluded that such pairs as 'bachelor' and 'unmarried man' are not synonymous, since one, but not the other, can occur in the context *-hood* etc. . . . But all that this observation shows is that the proposed criterion is entirely wrong, as, indeed, it clearly is.'[1] The issue between Chomsky and the distributionalist is irresolvable in that if the distributionalist is right then Chomsky's counterexample—or any other—must be mistaken. On the other hand, if the distributionalist thesis can be confirmed or refuted on the basis of examples or counterexamples, then it is both possible and necessary to establish synonymity independently of the distributional evidence. But the assumption that meanings determine distribution in such a way that difference in distribution is a sufficient condition of difference in meaning appears ultimately to involve what amounts to equation of 'meaning' with 'distribution', in which case the proposals concerning synonymy are trivial.

As regards 'quantification' of synonymy, it may be pointed out that drawing distinctions between various degrees of or approximations to synonymity on the basis of 'componential analysis' or 'semantic classification' (cf. Sparck Jones 1964) is in all essentials a continuation of the approach of the synonymists. But this approach presupposes rather than proposes answers to the questions we are trying to answer. It is evident that, given a system of semantic categorization, synonymous expressions will be those receiving identical characterizations under that system. Other degrees or varieties of synonymity can be duly distinguished if we wish. Weinreich proposes to call any pair of terms *A* and *A'* 'immediate synonyms' if their designata differ by one component.[2] Ducháček proposes a distinction between 'perfect synonyms', 'approximate synonyms', and 'words semantically related'; but concedes that there is room for disagreement over the criteria to be applied.[3] Abraham and Kiefer propose a distinction between 'full' and 'less-than-full' synonymy, with reference to tree diagrams representing the various grammatical and semantic categories of a word. According to their

---

[1] Chomsky 1962, p. 527. [2] Weinreich 1963, § 4.2.
[3] Ducháček 1964, Ducháček 1967 §§ 14—17.

definition, 'between two words, W_1 and W_2, a full synonymy holds if, and only if, their trees have exactly the same branching structure (i.e. the same paths) and exactly the same labels on the corresponding nodes', while 'an i-ways synonymy holds if, and only if, they have in their tree graphs i paths in common'. The various paths distinguish between different uses of the word in question; but if we ask how these uses are determined, all we are told is that they can be found 'recorded in any good explanatory dictionary'.[1] The point about all such proposals is that conditions of adequacy on any system of semantic categorization are imposed by considerations external to it. This means that instances of synonymity supply a criterion for the system, and not vice versa. If, for example, a semantic analysis is to be given of English terms for domestic animals, then *dog* and *cat* will turn out to be synonymous if 'quadruped' and 'carnivorous' are the only two relevant semantic labels the system provides. To say that this result shows the system to be absurdly inadequate is doubtless correct; but that can only be said if it can be determined independently that *dog* and *cat* are not synonymous.

Many questions concerning the concept 'linguistic meaning' will be left open in the discussion of synonymy to be presented. Unavoidably so; for if all the problems connected with the concept 'linguistic meaning' could be easily resolved, synonymy would hardly be a topic worth discussing. But to say this is not to deny that whoever leaves a question on one side—or fails to raise it—is committed by implication to the contention that his argument is not thereby seriously affected.

An earlier draft of the present study was submitted as a Ph.D. thesis at the University of London. The research was undertaken in the Department of Phonetics and Linguistics at the School of Oriental and African Studies under Professor C. E. Bazell, to whom the author's thanks are due for constant encouragement and lively criticism.

[1]Abraham & Kiefer 1966.

CHAPTER ONE

Synonymy, form and meaning

It is important to distinguish at the outset between two related
but separate issues: (i) whether or not any language could have
expressions differing in form but not in meaning, and (ii) whether
or not any language does have expressions differing in form but
not in meaning. The former is a matter of relations between
definitions, i.e. the only sense in which no language could have
expressions differing in form but not in meaning would be if we
chose to define 'form' and 'meaning' in such a way that it followed
from our definitions that any statement to the effect that expressions
a and *b* differed in form but not in meaning would be self-contradictory. If, on the other hand, we do not so define 'form' and
'meaning' the possibility is open that any language may have
expressions differing in form but not in meaning. The question
whether any language does have such expressions is a subordinate
question, in that whether it arises at all depends on the answer
propounded to the question of definitions.

Let us consider the following postulate:

(P1) The expressions of a language differ one from another in
form or meaning, but not necessarily in both.

That P1 constitutes a reasonable and, for purposes of linguistic
analysis, an indispensable minimal assumption may be concluded
from the following argument.

If a linguistic expression is regarded as an item characterized in
the dimensions of form and meaning, such that in order to recognize
instances of any expression it is necessary to know its form, and in
order to understand any expression it is necessary to know its meaning
then unless we treat some expressions in a language as having different
meanings from others, and some expressions as having different
forms from others, it becomes impossible to explain how a language
is successfully employed for purposes of communication. That is to
say, either of the assumptions (i) that all expressions of the language
have the same form, or, (ii) that all expressions of the language have
the same meaning, fails to provide a satisfactory basis on which

to account for the ways in which, by means of discourse, one language-user understands and can be understood by others. For on neither of the assumptions mentioned would difference in form be correlatable with difference in meaning. An analysis based on either would thus be unable in principle to account for the successful use of a language in communication situations.

It follows from the assumption that some expressions differ in form and some in meaning that at least some of those expressions differing in meaning will differ also in form.

Thus three possibilities are to be envisaged. First, there will be cases in which two expressions differ both in form and meaning. Second, there may be cases in which a difference of meaning between two expressions is not accompanied by a difference of form: in such cases we may speak of 'homonymous expressions'. Third, there may be cases in which a difference of form between two expressions is not accompanied by a difference of meaning: in such cases we may speak of 'synonymous expressions'.

The concept of synonymy thus takes its place in a framework of assumptions according to which any linguistic expression is taken to have both form and meaning, but in which sameness in respect of form does not imply sameness in respect of meaning, nor vice versa.

If P1 is accepted, the question of excluding the possibility of synonymous expressions arises only if it is maintained that linguistic analysis requires some further postulate or postulates compatible with P1 but precluding the possibility of difference in form without difference of meaning.

The view is advanced by Bloomfield[1] that linguistic analysis is based upon a postulate which requires us to suppose that within a given natural language there are no synonymous expressions. Bloomfield does not make out a detailed case, but the postulate in question is stated to be:

(P2) 'In certain communities (speech-communities) some speech-utterances are alike as to form and meaning.'

Bloomfield maintains (a) that this postulate obliges us to suppose that phonemic difference is invariably concomitant with difference of meaning, e.g. 'that each one of a set of forms like *quick, fast, swift, rapid, speedy* differs from all the others in some constant and con-

[1] Bloomfield 1935, § 9.5.

ventional feature of meaning', and (b) that the postulate implies that difference of meaning is compatible with phonemic identity, e.g. 'in English, the phonetic form [bɛə] occurs with three different meanings: *bear* 'to carry, to give birth to', *bear* 'ursus', and *bare* 'uncovered'.' Thus, according to Bloomfield, homonymity is possible, but synonymity excluded.

However, this conclusion does not in fact follow from the single postulate as Bloomfield formulates it, since the assertion that some utterances are alike in form and meaning does not preclude the possibility of synonymous expressions. There would be no difficulty in formulating a postulate which did, e.g.

(P3) The expressions of a language differ one from another in form or meaning, and if in form then also in meaning.

But the question which must be considered is whether there is any good reason for adopting a postulate such as P3.

Suppose we define the class K of communication systems as comprising all and only those in which any pair of expressions differing in form differ also in meaning, and, correspondingly the class K' as comprising all and only those containing at least one pair of expressions differing in form but not in meaning. Accepting P3 would commit us to including all natural languages in the class K.

The problem for the advocate of P3 is to explain why we should accept as valid for purposes of linguistic analysis a position which, as regards communication systems in general, is clearly untenable. For given a constructed language L belonging to K, we can specify a further language L' which includes L together with some additional expression e having the same meaning as one of the expressions of L. That is to say we can, in the case of constructed languages, arbitrarily modify the system by introducing synonymous expressions (as a government can introduce new coins having the same value as old coins, and so modify the existing currency system). Presumably Dr. Zamenhof might have decided, as a whimsical afterthought, to have two Esperanto words for 'electricity' instead of one. The committee responsible for the International Code of Signals might decide to introduce a new signal as an optional alternative to one of the existing signals. If it is denied that synonymous expressions can thus be created by fiat,[1] we must abandon the term 'synonymous expressions' as being tied to an inappropriate concept of meaning, and find some other way of talking about the relation in question. If not, then a

[1] Cf. Quine 1961 § 2.

test is available for assessing proposals which have the effect of rendering difference of form a sufficient condition of difference in meaning. The test will be whether the proposals can explain why no system of the type envisaged by the proposal could belong to K'; in other words, in the case of natural languages, why the language-giver —to borrow Plato's metaphor—could not have done what we presume to lie within the power of one who constructs any communication system.

No such explanation will be forthcoming on the basis of a definition of meaning which would simply preclude the possibility of communication systems not belonging to K, as e.g. if the meaning of an expression is defined as 'the total network of relations entered into' by that expression.[1] For if the meaning of a is the total network of relations entered into by a, and the meaning of b is the total network of relations entered into by b, and a and b are not one and the same expression, then the meaning of a must differ from the meaning of b. It follows that for any system L belonging to K we cannot, by introducing further formally distinct expressions, construct a system L' which is not a member of K. But what this shows is that the definition fails to capture 'meaning' in the sense relevant to the question at issue.[2]

The same test may be applied in cases where a proposal is not overtly based on any explicit definition of meaning. For example, under a proposal advanced by Goodman,[3] difference of form would be a sufficient condition of difference in meaning for any two extensional expressions in communication systems allowing the construction of compound expressions of a certain type. Goodman's point of departure is that identity of extension would be an adequate criterion of synonymity for most pairs of extensional expressions, at least if we were restricting our interest to such aspects of meaning as affect the truth or falsehood of assertions. Even so, a problem arises if we wish to include within the scope of our definition extensional expressions of which the extension is the null class. For according to

---

[1] This 'Firthian' definition is proposed in Catford 1965, § 5.1.

[2] The definition cited is intended to cover both what in Firthian terminology is called 'formal meaning' and also 'contextual meaning'. 'The various formal relations into which a form enters constitute its *formal meaning*' (Catford 1965, § 5.11). 'The contextual meaning of an item is the groupment of relevant situational features with which it is related' (Catford 1965, § 5.2). P3 would thus need reformulating in some such terms as: 'The expressions of a language differ one from another in formal meaning and contextual meaning, and if in formal meaning then also in contextual meaning.'

[3] Goodman 1949.

the criterion proposed, such expressions as *unicorn* and *mountain higher than Everest* would be synonymous, since they coincide in extension. But if it is the case that Mary thought she saw a unicorn in the garden, she would be telling the truth if she said 'I thought I saw a unicorn in the garden', but uttering a falsehood if she said 'I thought I saw a mountain higher than Everest in the garden'.

Goodman's resolution of this difficulty is to propose the following amendment of the suggested account of synonymy for extensional expressions. An expression such as *chair* may be regarded not only as having an extension in the usual sense, but also as having 'secondary extensions'. A secondary extension will be defined as the extension of a compound expression in which the expression *chair* appears as a constituent part, e.g. the expression *picture of a chair*. The amended criterion of synonymity proposed is: 'identity of primary and secondary extensions'. That is, *a* and *b* are synonymous if and only if they coincide not simply in respect of their extension in the usual sense, but also in respect of the extensions of all matching compounds which include *a* and *b* as parts. The amended criterion now seems adequate to cope with cases like *unicorn* and *mountain higher than Everest*, since there will be matching compounds (e.g. *picture of a unicorn* and *picture of a mountain higher than Everest*) which do not agree extensionally and thus rule them out as a synonymous pair.

However, acceptance of the amendment has the consequence that no two extensional expressions *a* and *b* can be regarded as synonymous. For the expression *chair that is not a stool* can be correctly applied to any chair but to no stool: it qualifies, so the argument runs, as a chair-description but not a stool-description. Thus the expressions *chair* and *stool* differ in secondary extension, for there are matching compounds, namely *chair-description* and *stool-description*, which differ in extension. Now in the expression *chair that is not a stool*, we might substitute for *chair* and *stool* any two nonequiform expressions *a* and *b*, and arrive at the same result. Whereas if we insert the same expression *a* in both places, we have an expression of the type *chair that is not a chair*—and such an expression, whatever its status, clearly cannot simultaneously be and not be a chair-description. The conclusion is that no two extensional expressions can be synonymous.

Goodman's proposal is found wanting, however, under a test of the kind proposed above. Let us suppose that *S* is a language belonging to K, having extensional expressions and the grammatical apparatus required under Goodman's proposal. Can we now construct a corresponding system S', analogous in all relevant respects, but with identical dictionary entries for some pair of extensional expressions having the null class as their extension? Not if we accept Goodman's criterion of synonymity. But to deny the possibility of S' is tantamount to claiming that not even in a fairy tale, or science fiction story, could an author invent a race of imaginary creatures and give them two alternative names (e.g. *trugs* or *bogglewits*) without *ipso facto* creating (provided the language had the grammatical apparatus for constructing 'trug-descriptions' and 'bogglewit-descriptions') two words with different meanings. Such a conclusion simply leaves one baffled as to the sense of the term 'meaning' here. For what the proposal does not explain is why anyone should accept failure to agree in secondary extension as a sufficient condition for difference of meaning between two expressions which coincide in primary extension and differ in secondary extension only in virtue of the fact that they differ in form. For example, granted that the words *furze* and *gorse* have the same primary extension, it seems that the case for saying that *furze that is not gorse* counts as a 'furze-description' but not as a 'gorse-description' rests ultimately upon formal features of that expression, i.e. 'furze-description' must here be explicated in some such fashion as 'description using the word *furze*. . . .' For if any other word than *furze* were used, then by Goodman's own argument we should not have a 'furze-description' that was not a 'gorse-description'. But if that is so, then all the difference in secondary extension assures us of is that *furze* and *gorse* differ in form, which was known at the outset. Furthermore, even as regards expressions having the null class as their extension, the proposal is defective. For while it supplies an 'extensional' explanation of the difference between, say, *unicorn* and *cockatrice*, it does so at the expense of not being able to account for the lack of difference between *cockatrice* and *basilisk*. A picture of a unicorn is not a picture of a cockatrice: but a picture of a cockatrice is a picture of a basilisk.

A more interesting denial of synonymity would be one based upon the thesis that a natural language, unlike a constructed language, is such that the conditions for synonymity of two expressions are never fulfilled. P3, it might be suggested, can be supported by an argument along the lines advanced by White,[1] which may be summarized as follows.

Synonymy is held to be sameness of meaning of different expressions. If this is correct, then to interpret aright claims that *a* is synonymous with *b* we need to clarify (i) the 'sameness' involved, and (ii) the 'meaning' involved.

(i) At least four different kinds of 'sameness' may be distinguished. We use the word 'same' in connexion with various parts of the history of one continuous thing. For example, to whatever position in the room a chair is moved, we still regard it as the same chair. We will correct an acquaintance who mistakenly supposes that the chair that used to stand by the window has been sold and that there is a new chair that stands by the door. 'No,' we say, 'it's the same chair.' Similarly, we refer to 'the same man we saw yesterday'. Such cases are examples of 'type-1 sameness'. Second, there is the kind of case in which we have two or more instances of non-continuous things ('type-2 sameness'), as when we talk about 'the same dance step' or 'the same experiment', alluding to a repetition of previous actions. Then there is the kind of case where we recognize sameness in two or more coexistent copies of one thing ('type-3 sameness'), as when we talk about 'the same newspaper', 'the same curtains', 'the same motor car' or 'the same gramophone record'. In such cases there may not be a prototype over and above the copies. Finally, there is the kind of case where we say that at least two continuous things are the same in a given respect ('type-4 sameness'), as when we tell someone that he has the same eyes, or the same bearing, or the same manner as his father. We use this formula even when the comparison between A and B hinges on a detachable object which is not part of them, as when we say 'they have the same room', meaning that they share it. There are, however, English idiomatic differences corresponding to this latter distinction. For if the respect in question is a non-detachable, non-interchangeable characteristic (like manner, limp, hair, or even—as a marginal case—income) it is usual to say not only that A and B 'have the same X', but also that they are 'alike in' or 'in respect of' X; whereas if the respect involves a detachable, interchangeable object (like room, car or hat) it is usual to say that A and B 'have the same X', but hardly that they are 'alike in' or 'in respect of ' X.

'Type-4 sameness' may be further analysed as follows. If A and

1 White 1958.

B

B are the same in respect of a given object, we may, classify the same-ness of that object under 'type-1 sameness' or 'type-3 sameness'. That is, it will either be one and the same object which A and B share (e.g. room or garden fence) or, on the other hand, there will be two distinct copies of the same sort (e.g. motor car). But the question of whether the object counts as one or two does not depend on how many possessors it has. However, if A and B are the same in respect of a given characteristic, it is not always easy to decide whether we are dealing with one characteristic or two, and the question of how many possessors it has becomes more important. There are two general arguments for classing such characteristics under 'type-3 sameness'. One is that it makes perfectly good sense to say in such cases that there is one X (e.g. limp, interest, hair-do) which A has, and another X which B has, but no difference between them. This is supported by the second argument, that it is possible for someone to know that both A and B have X, but not to recognize it as the same characteristic.

The sameness involved when it is claimed that two expressions 'have the same meaning' is 'type-4 sameness', i.e. the claim maintains that two given expressions a and b are the same in respect of X, their meaning. If we accept this, then the further question arises of assessing 'meaning' as a respect in which instances of 'sameness' may occur.

(ii) 'Meaning,' in the sense in which it may be claimed that two expressions 'have the same meaning', is most satisfactorily regarded as a characteristic in respect of which the expressions are the same. This characteristic is the way or ways in which the expressions are employed by language-users. Thus there are general arguments (see above) for classing the meaning which expressions share under 'type-3 sameness'.

But this conclusion is just the one which raises insuperable difficulties as far as determining synonymity is concerned. For 'type-3 sameness' for characteristics is the case where sameness is in the eye of the beholder, i.e. where there is no objectively verifiable 'same object' involved, and all depends on whether we choose to pay attention to the similarities and ignore the differences. It is typical of 'type-3 sameness' for characteristics that there is always some view-point from which two allegedly same respects can, in principle, be differentiated. Hence if we believe that there are instances where two expressions cannot be differentiated in respect of meaning, we must be deceiving ourselves. This is not to say that we shall not find instances where a plausible case can be made out for saying that two expressions are synonymous: but that the decision will be arbitrary, in the sense that there will always be—if we choose to look for it— some reason for denying that the meaning is 'the same'.

Thus the case of allegedly synonymous expressions is like that of the spanner and the wrench. We may say that a spanner and a wrench have the same use, namely to tighten and loosen nuts, or that they have different uses, because the way a spanner tightens a nut is not exactly the same as the way a wrench does, and besides there are other uses which wrenches have and spanners do not. Similarly, e.g. the expressions *brother* and *male sibling* may be alleged to be synonymous, and there is a good reason for this, namely that both are used to specify a certain family relationship. On the other hand, reasons may be found for denying that they are used in exactly the same way, e.g. that one expression provides a translation of the French word *frère*, while the other does not, or that one expression explicitly analyses the relationship in question, whereas the other does not. We thus have a choice of asserting or denying that these two expressions are synonymous, depending on whether we wish to call attention to the similarities of meaning, or the differences.

In general, the following are ways by one or other of which we may always differentiate between the meanings of any two expressions if we so wish: (a) by showing that the meaning of a is known to a person X, when the meaning of b is not; (b) by showing that the meaning of a may be rendered in some other language by an espression which is not an exact translation of b; (c) by showing that a differs in the organization of meaningful elements from b; (d) by showing that the meaning of a differs in some respect other than intension or extension (e.g. emotively) from the meaning of b; (e) by showing that a has for a person X associations not shared by b.

Thus there will always be something true of the meaning of a which is not true of the meaning of b, even in cases where some other consideration might induce us to say that the meanings of a and b were 'the same'.

White's position may be compared with that taken up by Nida, who holds that the non-occurrence of synonymous expressions in natural languages is a 'principle of semantic analysis'. In support of this contention, Nida observes that certain expressions 'ordinarily listed as synonyms' turn out, upon investigation, not to be identical in meaning. Examples are: *peace* and *tranquillity*, *childish* and *puerile*, *truth* and *reality*. This holds also, in Nida's view, for variant pronunciations of a given word:

> 'For example, the alternant pronunciations of *duty* (1)/duwtiy/ and (2)/dyuwtiy/ carry certain distinct connotations. In some circumstances the form /dyuwtiy/ induces an unfavorable response from the listener, who interprets it as pedantic or associated with people whose culture he does not appreciate. On the other hand, among a certain small set of speakers of American English the form /duwtiy/ is a mark of educational and cultural inferiority. The alternant pronunciations of *creek* /kriyk/ and /krik/ bear similar distinctions, but to different types of speakers. If alternant pronunciations of morphemes do nothing more than identify the dialect area, they are to that extent nonequivalent.'[1]

Thus according to both White and Nida close investigation of the use of expressions in a natural language will always reveal some reason for denying their synonymity.

But pointing out various ways of distinguishing between alleged synonyms is the traditional pastime of synonymists. Collinson lists nine possible differentiae:

'(1) One term is more general and inclusive in its applicability, another is more specific and exclusive, e.g. *refuse/reject*. Cf. *seaman/sailor*, *ending/inflexion*, *go on foot/march*.

(2) One term is more intense than another, e.g. *repudiate/refuse*. Cf. *immense/great*, *towering/tall*.

(3) One term is more highly charged with emotion than another, e.g. *repudiate* or *reject/decline*. Cf. *looming/emerging*, *louring/threatening*.

(4) One term may imply moral approbation or censure where another is neutral, e.g. *thrifty/economical*, *eavesdrop/listen*.

(5) One term is more "professional" than another; e.g. *calcium chloride/chloride of lime/bleaching powder*; *decease/death*; *domicile/house*; *to ordain a priest, institute* or *induct a vicar, consecrate* or *instal a bishop/appoint a professor*.

(6) One term belongs more to the written language, it is more literary than another, e.g. *passing/death*. The literary language includes further distinctions like the poetical and the archaic.

[1] Nida 1949 § 6.11.

(7) One term is more colloquial than another, e.g. *turn down/ refuse*. The spoken language, too, includes further distinctions like the familiar, slangy and vulgar.

(8) One term is more local or dialectal than another, e.g. Scots *flesher/butcher*, or *to feu/to let*.

(9) One term belongs to child-talk, is used by children or in talking to children, e.g. *daddy, dad, papa/father* (in which different social levels are discernible), *teeny/tiny*, etc.'[1]

Ingenuity might find ways of adding considerably to this list. But however long the list of differentiae, it will still fall short of providing the required support for P3, unless reason is shown for supposing that any pair of expressions must be differentiable on at least one such count.[2] For it would be a misapplication of Leibniz's law to proceed on the assumption that establishing that something is true of the meaning of *a* which is not true of the meaning of *b* is sufficient to show that *a* and *b* differ in meaning.[3] To clinch White's argument, it would need to be shown that the various criteria for synonymity are interrelated in such a way that any pair of natural-language expressions satisfying one or some of these criteria necessarily fail to satisfy another or others. This final step in the argument is the step missing.

The case presented thus far in favour of accepting P1 but rejecting P3 has assumed that the concept of synonymous expressions in a constructed language was an unexceptionable one, and this was the basis for scepticism about P3. The defender of P3, it was suggested, would need to explain why the assumption that difference in form

---

[1] Collinson 1939, pp. 61–62. The analysis is based on that given by Devoto in the article 'Sinonomia' in the *Enciclopedia Italiana*, Vol. XXXI, p. 857. Cf. Baldinger 1970 II,5.

[2] This applies whether or not we accept the validity of particular differentiae. E.g. one might question the assumption, apparently accepted by Collinson, Nida and White, that to establish that different speakers have different attitudes to the use of *a* and *b* is sufficient to establish that *a* and *b* differ in meaning. (This leads Ziff (Ziff 1960, § 179 n. 3) to dismiss Nida's conclusion that natural languages do not have synonyms as based on a confusion between 'meaning' and 'connotation'.)

[3] Analogously, one could never conclude that two articles in a shop cost the same, since certain things might be true of the price of one article which were not true of the price of the other, e.g. that one price had been determined by the shop manager and the other by the wholesaler, or that one price was regarded by the customer as cheap, and the other as dear, etc. But to anyone who argued thus, it would be correct to reply: these are certainly possible ways of differentiating between the two prices, but they have nothing to do with establishing whether or not the prices are the same.

was a sufficient condition of difference in meaning was a valid assumption for natural languages, although manifestly incorrect in the case of constructed languages. In support of this position, the concept of synonymous expressions in a constructed language requires some clarification, and a fuller account of its relevance to the question of synonymy in natural languages must be provided.

We may begin by pointing out that all that has so far been taken for granted about 'form' and 'meaning' is that it is in virtue of knowing the form of an expression that language-users are able to recognize instances of that expression, and in virtue of knowing the meaning of an expression that they are able to understand it when used in discourse. These assumptions fit equally well the case of a natural language or of a constructed sign system of any kind.

As regards natural languages, a distinction between formal and semantic knowledge answers to certain elementary criteria one would apply in assessing language learning. For example, a Frenchman learning English might be taught the correct pronunciation or spelling of the word *eight*; but one would not wish to say that he knew the meaning of the word simply on the basis of his success in recognizing tokens of the type, or producing such tokens himself when called upon to do so. Or, on the other hand, he might be taught that there was an English word for the cardinal number '8', and he might even be taught, by means of partial translations with blanks, where that word ought to occur in English sentences as an equivalent of French *huit*. He might perhaps then be described as knowing the meaning of a certain English word; but one would not wish to say he knew the form of the word in question until he knew e.g. how to fill in the blanks translating French *huit*.

The distinction also matches different ways in which one would describe features of success or failure in language-using. For example, if I have temporarily forgotten the name of the small Hampshire village where my Aunt May lives, and so cannot comply with your request for her address, it is a form, not a meaning, which I cannot recall. But it is a meaning not a form which I have (partially) forgotten if I used to know the definition of *typhlitis*, but cannot now remember whether the term applies to cases of appendicitis or not.

Thus a distinction between formal and semantic knowledge may be supported in various ways. These may be paralleled in the case of constructed sign systems even of a very elementary kind; for example, the 'builder's language' described by Wittgenstein in § 2 of the

Philosophische Untersuchungen.[1] One might in such a case describe the relevant linguistic knowledge by specifying (i) what patterns of articulated sound count as instances of utterance of the expressions *Würfel, Säule, Platte* and *Balken,* and (ii) what requirement the utterance of each of these expressions indicates. For this is the knowledge which would enable anyone to assume the role either of the builder or of his assistant in the communication situation envisaged. All that falls under (i) comprises formal knowledge, and all that falls under (ii) semantic knowledge. Someone might have the requisite formal knowledge without the requisite semantic knowledge, e.g. he might be able to recognize utterances of *Würfel, Säule, Platte* and *Balken,* but not know, or be mistaken about, which kind of item was to be brought in response to which kind of utterance. This is to be distinguished from not knowing the difference between utterances of *Würfel, Säule* etc.

From the point of view of an outside observer trying to construct a hypothesis about the linguistic knowledge shared by the builder and his assistant, it would suffice to 'set up' four linguistic expressions, each differing from the others both in 'form' (i.e. in respect of what sound sequences count as utterances of the expression) and in 'meaning' (i.e. in respect of what requirement the utterance of the expression indicates).

This situation is in all essentials that of the linguist engaged in the description of a natural language. From his point of view, linguistic expressions may be defined as theoretical constructs set up as units in terms of which to state linguistic knowledge, this knowledge being postulated to account for interpersonal communication by speech or writing.

The mechanism of explanation based upon such constructs is typically as follows. If on a given occasion A communicates successfully with B by uttering a certain sequence of sounds, we explain this by supposing that B's linguistic knowledge enables him to recognize the sounds as a token of a certain type, and, in virtue of belonging to that type, as being understandable in a certain way. We also suppose that A's linguistic knowledge enables him to select the appropriate

---

[1] 'Die Sprache soll der Verständigung eines Bauenden A mit einem Gehilfen B dienen. A führt einen Bau auf aus Bausteinen; es sind Würfel, Säulen, Platten und Balken vorhanden. B hat ihm die Bausteine zuzureichen, und zwar nach der Reihe, wie A sie braucht. Zu dem Zweck bedienen sie sich einer Sprache, bestehend aus den Wörtern: "Würfel", "Säule", "Platte", "Balken". A ruft sie aus;—B bringt den Stein, den er gelernt hat, auf diesen Ruf zu bringen.—Fasse dies als vollständige primitive Sprache auf.' (Wittgenstein 1958).

sequence of sounds to utter, on the assumption that B would recognize them as a token of the type in question, and understand accordingly.[1] *Mutatis mutandis*, similar suppositions apply in the case where A communicates with B by means of marks on a surface, or other visual as opposed to auditory signals. Communication is explained, in short, by supposing that acts of communication (speech acts, acts of writing) involve the instantiation of linguistic expressions by A, and B's application of his own linguistic knowledge to their recognition and interpretation.

For each linguistic expression set up, therefore, a specification is required of both 'form' and 'meaning'. A language *L* may be described by specifying a set of linguistic expressions, each character-ized in respect of form and meaning.

Clearly, it does not advance the explanation of communication-in-*L* to multiply 'linguistic expressions' unnecessarily. If different linguistic expressions of *L* (the language under description) are to be set up to accommodate various formal and semantic distinctions, when we speak of two linguistic expressions, it is implied that there is a difference in form or in meaning, or both. If there is no difference in form or in meaning, there is no sense in which two linguistic expressions are involved, as distinct from two instantiations of the same expression. This proviso corresponds to the way in which rules are to be envisaged as governing a constructed communication system. E.g. it would be nonsense for Wittgenstein's builder and his assistant to agree (a) that *Balken* was the word to be uttered by the builder when he wanted a beam brought, and furthermore (b) that the requirement of a beam by the builder was to be indicated by his uttering the word *Balken*. To agree to both (a) and (b) would be merely to reiterate agreement to one and the same rule (i.e. the rule for the expression *Balken*), not to set up rules for the two expressions *Balken* and *Balken*.

To create synonymous expressions in a constructed language would be to agree that one and the same semantic rule should apply to two or more expressions recognized as distinct. E.g. the builder and his assistant, dissatisfied with Wittgenstein's meagre and unimaginative provision for their intercourse, might agree that (a) the requirement of a beam by the builder might be indicated by his

---

[1]Attempts at the elucidation of various details of the concept of communication between speaker and hearer are to be found in Grice 1957, 1968 and 1969, Strawson 1964, Searle 1969.

uttering the word *Balken*, and that furthermore (b) alternatively, the very same requirement might also be indicated by his uttering the word *Austerlitz*. And they might proceed to agree upon using the names of other famous battles as optional alternatives to the other words, thus providing each of the expressions *Würfel*, *Säule*, *Platte* and *Balken* with a synonym. (They would thus be instituting rules in a manner no different from the mathematician who stipulates (i) 'Let the value of x be 3' and (ii) 'Let the value of y be 3'; nor from the logician who sets up an interpreted logistic system in which 'F' and 'G' are constants standing for the same two-place predicate, so that 'Fab' and 'Gab' are both interpreted as 'a is the father of b'.) Correspondingly, the linguist constructing a hypothesis about the builder's language, based on observation of its use, would be led to set up *Balken* and *Austerlitz* as synonymous expressions in order to account for the fact that the communicational purpose served by both words appeared to be the same.

From this point of view, the concept of synonymy may be considered part of the structure of explanatory hypotheses about communication-in-L.

Showing that synonymy is a realizable relation in respect of constructed languages does not in itself constitute a case for supposing that natural languages have synonymous expressions. But it does put the onus on those who would reject any synonymy postulate for linguistic analysis, e.g.

(SP) There may be pairs of expressions of L which differ in form
     but not in meaning

to argue for the rejection.

Two further points emerge. First, acceptance of SP would make available explanatory hypotheses of a certain structure concerning possible processes of communication between speakers of L. Second, constructed language analogues show in general what sort of sense to make of the question: 'how would acceptance of SP affect the descriptive linguistic analysis of natural languages?'

'Es zerstreut den Nebel, wenn wir die Erscheinungen der Sprache an primitiven Arten ihrer Verwendung studieren, in denen man den Zweck und das Funktionieren der Wörter klar übersehen kann.' But the fog is dispersed at the cost of oversimplification. The less complex the internal organization of L, and the more limited the range of communication situations in which L is used, the clearer will be the application of a distinction between expressions which differ in meaning and those which do not. We may expect matters to be complicated in the case of natural languages by (i) the formal complexity of natural languages, (ii) the semantic complexity of natural languages, and (iii) the fact that the scope and purpose of communicational exchanges may be far less clearly demarcated than in the use of a restricted sign system of a very simple kind.

CHAPTER TWO

Synonymy and Phonological Analysis

To what extent does the possibility that there may be L-synonymous expressions affect the enterprise of giving a phonological description of L?

This question may be raised quite independently of the question as to what systematization should be employed in stating the descriptive phonology of a language. It therefore cuts across such controversial issues as the justification of 'autonomous phonology'.[1] For, irrespective of the descriptive systematization adopted, a phonological account of L must fully reflect the communicationally relevant sound distinctions made and recognized by speakers of L.

It happens, however, that questions of synonymy have most frequently been raised in the context of the debate between critics and defenders of what may conveniently be called 'semantically based phonology'. This is of some relevance for present purposes in that if the critics of semantically based phonology are right it would follow that acceptance of the synonymy postulate precludes the adoption of certain procedures and definitions in phonological analysis. But what is of most interest here is the broader theoretical import of the arguments on both sides, rather than the particular phonological procedures and definitions under discussion.

The general answer to the question 'To what extent does the possibility that there may be L-synonymous expressions affect the enterprise of giving a phonological description of L?' is, clearly enough, 'To the extent that the assignment of a particular phonological form or 'systematic phonetic' representation to an expression is not independent of the assignment of a meaning identical with, or differing from, that of other expressions of L'. What needs to be considered is whether there is an interdependence between the two, and if so what kind of interdependence it is.

By 'semantically based phonology' is here meant the view that the basis for phonological classification of the sounds of a language is the extent to which meanings of words, phrases or sentences in the

[1] Postal 1968.

language remain invariant under sound substitution, phonologically distinctive and non-distinctive sounds being distinguished in terms of the possibilities of interchange without change of meaning. It is characteristic of semantically based phonology to define phonological units, such as the phoneme, in such a way as to involve an appeal to meanings, whereas it is characteristic of nonsemantically based phonology to deny that appeal to meanings enters into such definitions.[1] It is assumed in semantically based phonology that at least some semantic information is essential for phonological analysis, whereas it is claimed by the advocates of nonsemantically based phonology that, at least in principle, correct phonological analysis is possible without semantic information.[2] For nonsemantically based phonology, therefore, questions of synonymy do not arise.

Arguments invoking synonymy have sometimes been advanced as reasons for rejecting semantically based phonology, and these merit examination in the present context.

According to Chomsky,[3] 'the central objection to meaning as a criterion of analysis has always been the obscurity of semantic notions' and synonymy is 'the most dubious part' of semantic theory. We must therefore realize what we are conceding if we claim 'that in order to construct a phonemic system it is necessary to know which utterances are different in meaning. To know difference in meaning is to know synonymy, and this is the central term of the theory of meaning. If accepted, then, this claim is an open admission that linguistic analysis must be based on precisely the most dubious part of semantic theory.' This general objection is backed up by more specific theoretical and methodological considerations. Semantically based phonology is represented by Chomsky as entailing acceptance of a particular 'synonymity criterion',[4] namely

<hr/>

[1] '... the phoneme is essentially a phonetic conception. The fact that certain sounds are used in a language for distinguishing the meanings of words doesn't enter into the definition of a phoneme.' D. Jones *Le Maître Phonétique* 3.7.44 (1929): quoted in Bloch 1948, p. 5.

[2] 'It would be possible to group the sounds of a language into phonemes without knowing the meaning of any words': D. Jones *loc. cit.* 'It is certainly possible to establish phonemic systems without having recourse to meaning at all': Ebeling 1960, p. 83. Bloch admits the utility of semantic information for the phonologist 'as a short cut in the investigation of phonemic structure' but insists on the possibility in principle of dispensing with it—with, however, one important proviso: 'Theoretically it would be possible to arrive at the phonemic system of a dialect entirely on the basis of phonetics and distribution, without any appeal to meaning—provided that in the utterances of the dialect not all the possible combinations of phonemes actually occurred': Bloch 1948, p. 5, n. 8.

[3] Chomsky 1955, pp. 141–142.   [4] Chomsky 1957, p. 95, n. 3.

SC1 'two utterances are phonemically distinct if and only if they differ in meaning'[1]

or, in an alternative and somewhat more exact formulation,

SC2 'given two utterance tokens U1 and U2, U1 is phonemically distinct from U2 if and only if U1 differs in meaning from U2'.[2]

The interpretation of the 'synonymity criterion' as applying to utterance tokens is stressed; SC1 'cannot be accepted, as it stands, as a definition of phonemic distinctness. If we are not to beg the question', the utterances in question must be tokens, not types.'[3] However, explicated thus the 'synonymity criterion' is open to the fundamental objection that 'there are utterance tokens that are phonemically distinct and identical in meaning (synonyms) and there are utterance tokens that are phonemically identical and different in meaning (homonyms).'[4] The proposed criterion is therefore 'false in both directions'.[5] Specific counterexamples cited are the following. 'Let U1 be the utterance *I saw him by the bank*, meaning the bank of the river, and let U2 be the utterance *I saw him by the bank*, i.e. the First National Bank. Clearly the two utterances are different in meaning. Nevertheless they are phonemically identical. Thus it is not the case that if U1 and U2 differ in meaning, then they must be phonemically distinct. Notice that we cannot appeal here to the fact that these physically distinct utterances are two occurrences of the same sentence, two tokens of the same type, because the problem at issue is precisely to determine which utterances (i.e. which distinct pieces of tape) are repetitions of one another or tokens of the same type. To make this appeal is thus to beg the question at issue completely.'[6] Synonyms provide counterexamples falsifying the 'synonymity criterion' in the other respect mentioned. 'Let U1 and U2 be any two expressions with the same meaning, e.g. 'he is a bachelor' and 'he is an unmarried man'. Or, if one is inclined to deny the existence of absolute synonyms, consider such pairs as/ekənamiks/ and /iykənamiks/, 'ádult' and 'adúlt', 'advértisement' and 'advertíse-ment', /ræšən/ and /reyšən/, /rædiyeytər/ and /reydiyeytər/, etc., which often coexist in one person's speech and are clearly synonyms. Such pairs have the same meanings but are phonemically distinct. Hence it is not the case that if two utterances are phonemically

---

[1] Chomsky 1957, p. 94.   [2] Chomsky 1955, p. 143.   [3] Chomsky 1957, p. 95.
[4] Chomsky 1957, p. 95.   [5] Chomsky 1955, p. 143: Chomsky 1957, p. 95.
[6] Chomsky 1955, p. 143. Another homonymous counterexample cited in Chomsky 1957, p. 95, is that of ' "metal" and "medal" (in many dialects)'.

distinct, then they must differ in meaning.'[1] It is thus clear, in Chomsky's view, that if we adopt the synonymity criterion 'we simply get the wrong classification in a large number of cases'.[2] He rejects in advance the defence that such cases are simply exceptions. 'We cannot circumvent this argument by holding that this rule . . . holds for all cases except the rather special case of homonyms and synonyms. For one thing, these are by no means peripheral cases. For another, 'homonymity' and 'synonymity' are simply the names we give to exceptions to this rule, and any rule works except for its exceptions.'[3]

Having argued against a semantically based definition of phonemic distinctness, Chomsky also attacks on similar grounds the thesis that the phonologist in practice requires semantic information in order to determine phonemic contrasts. 'Lounsbury argues in his 'A semantic analysis of the Pawnee kinship usage', *Language* 32.158-94 (1956), p. 190, that appeal to synonymity is necessary to distinguish between free variation and contrast: 'If a linguist who knows no English records from my lips the word *cat* first with a final aspirated stop and later with a final preglottalized unreleased stop, the phonetic data will not tell him whether these forms contrast or not. It is only when he asks me, his informant, whether the meaning of the first form is different from that of the second, and I say it is not, that he will be able to proceed with his analysis.' As a general method, this approach is untenable. Suppose that the linguist records /ekinamiks/ and /iykinamiks/, /viksin/ and /fiymeyl#faks/, etc., and asks whether or not they are different in meaning. He will learn that they are not, and will incorrectly assign them the same phonemic analysis, if he takes this position literally. On the other hand, there are many speakers who do not distinguish 'metal' from 'medal', though if asked, they may be quite sure that they do. The responses of such informants to Lounsbury's direct question about meaning would no doubt simply becloud the issue.

'We can make Lounsbury's position more acceptable by replacing the question 'do they have the same meaning?' with 'are they the same word?' This will avoid the pitfalls of the essentially irrelevant semantic question, but it is hardly acceptable in this form, since it amounts to asking the informant to do the linguist's work; it replaces an operational test of behavior (such as the pair test) by an inform-

---

[1] Chomsky 1955, pp. 143–144.   [2] Chomsky 1957, p. 95.
[3] Chomsky 1955, p. 144.

ant's judgment about his behavior. The operational tests for linguistic notions may require the informant to respond, but not to express his opinion about his behavior, his judgment about synonymy, about phonemic distinctness, etc. The informant's opinions may be based on all sorts of irrelevant factors. This is an important distinction that must be carefully observed if the operational basis for grammar is not to be trivialized.'[1]

As a nonsemantic method of determining phonemic contrast, Chomsky advocates the 'pair test' in the following form. 'Suppose that a linguist is interested in determining whether or not "metal" and "medal" are phonemically distinct in some dialect of English. He will not investigate the meanings of these words, since this information is clearly irrelevant to his purpose. He knows that the meanings are different (or he is simply not concerned with the question) and he is interested in determining whether or not the words are phonemically distinct. A careful field worker would probably use the pair test, either with two informants or with an informant and a tape recorder. For example, he might make a random sequence of copies of the utterance tokens that interest him, and then determine whether or not the speaker can consistently identify them. If there is consistent identification, the linguist may apply an even stricter test, asking the speaker to repeat each word several times, and running the pair test over again on the repetitions. If consistent distinguishability is maintained under repetition, he will say that the words "metal" and "medal" are phonemically distinct. The pair test with its variants and elaborations provides us with a clear operational criterion in completely non-semantic terms.'[2] This holds true, in Chomsky's view, even if the informant is asked to distinguish the utterance tokens in terms of meaning. 'One should not be confused by the fact that the subject in the pair test may be asked to identify the utterance tokens by meaning. He might just as well be asked to identify them by arbitrarily chosen numbers, by signs of the zodiac, etc. We can no more use some particular formulation of the pair test as an argument for dependence of grammatical theory on meaning than as an argument that linguistics is based on arithmetic or astrology.'[3]

Chomsky examines, and also rejects, a somewhat different version of the 'synonymity criterion'. 'A weaker claim . . . might be advanced

---

[1] Chomsky 1957, p. 97, n. 1.   [2] Chomsky 1957, pp. 96–97.
[3] Chomsky 1957, p. 99, n.1.

as follows. Suppose that we have an absolute phonetic system given in advance of any language, and guaranteed to be detailed enough so that every two phonemically distinct utterances in any language will be differently transcribed. It may now be the case that certain different tokens will be identically transcribed in this phonetic transcription. Suppose that we define the "ambiguous meaning" of an utterance token as the set of meanings of all tokens transcribed identically with this utterance token.' It might now be proposed that two utterances are phonemically distinct if and only if they differ in 'ambiguous meaning'. Chomsky concedes that such a proposal 'might provide an approach to the homonymity problem, if we had an immense corpus in which we could be fairly sure that each of the phonetically distinct forms of a given word occurred with each of the meanings that this word might have. It may be possible to elaborate this approach even further to cope with the problem of synonyms. In such a way one might hope to determine phonemic distinctness by laborious investigation of the meanings of phonetically transcribed items in a vast corpus. The difficulty of determining in any precise and realistic manner how many meanings several items may have in common, however, as well as the vastness of the undertaking, make the prospect for any such approach appear rather dubious.'[1]

Apart from the practical difficulties involved, Chomsky advances a further reason for rejecting the attempt to elaborate a semantically based phonology. 'There is one further difficulty of principle that should be mentioned in the discussion of any semantic approach to phonemic distinctness. We have not asked whether the meanings assigned to distinct (but phonemically identical) tokens are identical, or merely very similar. If the latter, then all of the difficulties of determining phonemic distinctness are paralleled (and magnified, because of the inherent obscurity of the subject matter) in determining sameness of meaning. We will have to determine when two distinct meanings are sufficiently similar to be considered 'the same'. If, on the other hand, we try to maintain the position that the meaning of a word is a fixed and unchanging component of each occurrence, then a charge of circularity seems warranted. It seems that the only way to uphold such a position would be to conceive of the meaning of a token as 'the way in which tokens of this type are (or can be) used,' the class of situations in which they can be used, the type of response that they normally evoke, or something of this

---

[1] Chomsky 1957, pp. 95–96.

sort. But it is difficult to make any sense at all out of such a conception of meaning without a prior notion of utterance type. It would appear, then, that even apart from our earlier objections, any approach to phonemic distinctness in semantic terms is either circular or is based on a distinction that is considerably more difficult to establish than the distinction it is supposed to clarify.'[1]

Chomsky's thesis may be considered as falling into two parts, one concerned with the definition of phonological units, the other with discovery procedures for the determination of such units in particular languages. Both parts involve arguments which invoke the concept of synonymy, and the arguments in question are in both cases open to objections, which must now be examined.

A general objection which may be raised against Chomsky's thesis concerns the alleged difficulty of semantic investigations, and, in particular, of establishing cases of synonymity. It is doubtless true that if one does not have a clear concept of synonymy, one will find it difficult to establish criteria for instances of synonymity: but this trivial observation applies equally to the concept of phonemic distinctness and to any other concept. Quite a different question is the question whether an investigator who *does* have a clear concept of synonymy, or of meaning, or of any other semantic concept, will find it difficult to establish criteria because the concepts in question are *semantic* concepts. Chomsky's arguments appear to assume an affirmative answer to this question, but the case for this answer is never satisfactorily made out. The use of phrases such as 'inherent obscurity' seems to suggest the existence of some fundamental difficulty attaching to semantic concepts, but the nature of the difficulty is never made clear. In practice, there would appear to be no greater order of difficulty involved in establishing whether a and b differ in meaning than in establishing whether a and b are phonemically distinct, granted the possibility of carrying out practical tests with informants. If an investigator has a clear concept of the semantic information he wishes to elicit, there seems no general reason why, either in principle or in practice, he may not devise testing techniques to elicit it.[2] In the particular case of testing for sameness of meaning

---

[1] Chomsky 1957, p. 98.
[2] Such techniques need not be open to the kind of objection Chomsky raises against Lounsbury's direct question about meaning.

C

of utterance tokens, Chomsky raises an objection which reveals a misconception of the question at issue; for, he alleges, such tests are complicated by the possibility of recognizing various 'degrees' of similarity of meaning. The assumption is, clearly, that unless we have a prior theory of synonymy which settles this and similar issues, then we do not know what we are testing for. But the 'difficulty' Chomsky raises is an irrelevance. No semantically based phonologist need waste time wondering whether, because ['laijǝn] and ['taigǝ] in a particular context appear to relate to very similar animals, he ought to count the meanings as 'the same'; nor, *mutatis mutandis*, for any other 'semantic similarity'. In phonology, the theoretical question 'how similar' meanings must be to be 'the same' simply does not arise: all the phonologist need be concerned with is establishing whether or not, in that context, his informants make a distinction. If they do, then ['laijǝn] and ['taigǝ] count as 'different': if not, they count as 'the same'.

The strategy of Chomsky's argument against the hypothetical defender of the 'synonymity criterion' contains a number of other unsatisfactory features, of which the most relevant for present purposes concern the implausibility of Chomsky's concept of synonymy. It appears that Chomsky wants to include under the term 'synonymy' any type of instance where one utterance-token is —in some sense—assigned the same meaning as some other utterance-token, as well as meaning-equivalence of corresponding types. What exactly is involved in assigning meanings is left unclarified, but Chomsky's examples include very disparate types of case. If mere instances where there is a variation of linguistic norm as regards the pronunciation of an expression (e.g. /ekinámiks/, /iykinámiks/) count as synonyms, they must be synonyms of a quite different kind from *vixen* and *female fox*. For while someone might just conceivably ask '*Is* /ekinámiks/ *the same subject as* /iykinámiks/?', no-one, unless he were joking, would give the definition '/ekinámiks/ *is* /iykinámiks/'. Whereas a quite standard way of defining 'vixen' is to say: '*A vixen is a female fox*'. It seems, therefore, that before one could profitably discuss the 'synonymity criterion' and its intended application, various distinctions would need clarification, including the following.

At least three types of question about meaning may be asked in respect of a given utterance-token. (1) We may be asked to identify the meaning of a given utterance-token in terms of the meaning or meanings assigned to a corresponding utterance-type: e.g. '*Does pink* here used of a newspaper mean *pink* as regards the colour of the paper it is printed on, or *pink* as regards the political views it expresses?'. (2) We may be asked to identify the meaning of an utterance-token by specifying the paradigm of non-anomalous semantic choices available in the context, and indicating which possibilities are excluded by the occurrence of the token in question. E.g. 'He rang off, replaced the receiver, and walked out of the telephone——.' What meanings does *kiosk* here exclude?' (Answer: *kiosk* here excludes 'booth', 'room', etc. N.B. The context already excludes 'wire', 'engineer', 'call' and other meanings which might otherwise go with *telephone*.) (3) We may be further asked to specify, in as great detail as may be required, the actual interpretation of that semantic choice, i.e. we may be required to elucidate in full, paying due attention to the speaker, place, time and social setting of the occasion, the implications which the utterance-token would have— and have been intended to have—for the audience to which it was addressed. E.g. 'What speed/length of time taken was implied by *fast journey* in that context?'

It will be relevant to the following discussion to distinguish by referring to questions of types (2) and (3) as questions of 'token-meaning' and questions of type (1) as questions of 'type-meaning classification'. These designations are intended to point to the fact that (1), although ostensibly a question about the meaning of the utterance-token, is in fact a disguised question about (exemplification of) a type-meaning.[1] This is expedient in order to avoid confusion arising between questions about the meaning of an utterance-token, and questions about the meaning of an utterance-type, which are categorically quite different questions. For to ask about the meaning of an utterance-token is to ask about a particular spatio-temporally unique event; whereas to ask about the meaning of an utterance-type is to ask about an abstraction which may correspond to very many particular events, or to none.

Now Chomsky is insistent that the 'synonymity criterion' must be interpreted as a thesis about the meanings of utterance-tokens. But his own use of the term *synonymity* and its cognates appears to cover (and thus fails to differentiate) at least three kinds of equivalence: (a)

---

[1] Question (1) asks, in effect, 'Which of *pink*-type's two meanings does this *pink*-token bear?'. Whereas (2) does not ask 'Which of *kiosk*-type's two (three...) meanings does this *kiosk*-token bear?' Nor does (3) ask 'Which of *fast*-type's two (three...) meanings does this *fast*-token bear?': for '80 m.p.h.' is not a meaning of the English type *fast*.

token-meaning equivalence, (b) type-meaning classification equivalence, and (c) equivalence in meaning of utterance-types.[1] For present purposes this would not matter much if (a) and (b) entailed (c), and likewise 'not (a)' and 'not (b)' both entailed 'not (c)'. But it is important to note that neither set of implications holds.[2]

It might of course be argued that if there were *no* instances where the meaning of a token *x* was identical with the meaning of a token *y*, then we should have no grounds for calling the corresponding types *X* and *Y* synonyms at all. But this is a consideration which cannot be advanced in Chomsky's favour, since the claim he makes is that the existence of certain synonymous expressions in some varieties of English 'falsifies' (sic) the 'synonymity criterion'. But the synonymous expressions cited are types (/ekinámiks/, /iykinámiks/ etc.), whereas the 'synonymity criterion', as already noted, is said to be a thesis about tokens. The assumption that one can argue from synonymity of types to equivalence of meaning of tokens simply begs the question against the defender of the 'criterion' since, obviously, no grounds have been advanced for claiming that some particular token [ekinámiks] has the same meaning as some other token [iykinámiks], other than the (alleged) synonymity of the corresponding types. The most that can be made of Chomsky's case on this point would seem to be some such assertion as the following: 'I am inclined to believe that in some varieties of English instances could be found where a token [ekinámiks] would prove to have no difference in meaning from another token [iykinámiks].'

But all our attention is being drawn to here is a phenomenon of speech variation. No such instance will 'falsify' the 'synonymity criterion', any more than instances of dialect mixture or bilingualism 'invalidate' the enterprise of phonological analysis. To contend otherwise is simply to confuse the notions 'false' and 'inapplicable'.[3] In cases like [ekinámiks]/ [iykinámiks] the investigator will conclude, if his researches are sufficiently extensive, that one or other pro-

---

[1] E.g. 'there are utterance tokens that are phonemically distinct and identical in meaning (synonyms)' and—in the same paragraph—'such absolute synonyms as /ekinamiks/ and /iykinamiks/.' (Chomsky 1957, p. 95). The former use of *synonym* seems to cover either (a) or (b), or perhaps both, while the latter corresponds to (c).

[2] The token-meaning equivalence of *x* and *y* does not entail the synonymity of types *X* and *Y*, nor vice-versa. Similarly, the synonymity of types *X* and *Y* does not entail and is not entailed by the type-meaning classification equivalence of *x* and *y*.

[3] Cf. Jones 1962 § 647: 'The speech of those whose pronunciation is unstable cannot be reduced to phonemes at all.' This is not an admission that the assumptions of phonology are false, but simply that their applicability is limited.

nunciation of the word must be excluded as intrusive. Or, if we insist that both be included within the same phonological description, we must clearly allow him to mark the two pronunciations, along with any similar hesitations for *equivalent, eclectic, effectual*, etc., as variants. We cannot expect the 'synonymity criterion', or any other proposed phonological criterion, to be capable of consistent application if we suppose the data to include phonologically incompatible realizations of expressions.[1] No linguistic criterion is deemed to hold for *whatever* data the linguist happens to have in front of him: all that is required is that it hold for all data conforming to a single linguistic norm.[2]

It might be urged on Chomsky's behalf that no such explanation is available for cases like [viksin] and [fiymeyl faks], supposing that instances could be found where two such tokens did not differ in meaning. But this brings us to a point which raises the question why Chomsky has selected a hypothetical opponent who is not in fact a phonologist at all but a lunatic, i.e. someone who is, apparently, proposing to make a phonological analysis of English with total disregard for any phonetic similarities or dissimilarities between items in the data. One does not wish to defend the views of lunatics. On the other hand, refuting them is of no great interest.[3] If the argument is intended as a *reductio ad absurdum* it fails, since non-semantically based phonology which ignored phonetic similarities and differences would be equally absurd.

Next, it must be observed that Chomsky's claim against the

[1] It might perhaps be argued that [ekinámiks] and [iykinámiks] do belong to the same phonological system in the sense of being statable in terms of different sequences of phonemes drawn from the same (English) inventory. But this is a contingent fact which does not affect the issue: the case is in principle no different from one in which a speaker sometimes does and sometimes does not observe a certain phonemic distinction.

[2] There is no presumption that collecting material from one informant guarantees its linguistic uniformity. The irrelevance of Chomsky's objection is indicated by the fact that if the data include speech variations which remain undetected the resultant phonological analysis will be 'wrong' regardless of whether the criteria used are semantic or non-semantic; e.g. if we ask an informant to pronounce *economics* on various occasions and, receiving sometimes the answer [ekinámiks] and sometimes the answer [iykinámiks], conclude that [e] and [iy] are members of the same phoneme. Naturally, if the phonologist thinks that *by using semantic criteria* he will automatically avoid the problem of speech variation he is mistaken. But that is a quite different matter (and a claim which, in any case, no advocate of semantically based phonology makes).

[3] This would hardly excuse anyone from regarding the lunatic's thesis as one open to refutation by counterexample, which it is not. Qua counterexample, [viksin]/[fiymeyl faks] is just as vain as [ekinámiks]/[iykinámiks]. (It would be equally vain to argue against someone who said 'A triangle has four sides' by claiming 'I can show you some which have only three.')

'criterion' is that it is false both (i) as a necessary condition of phonemic distinctness (against which he adduces synonyms), and also (ii) as a sufficient condition of phonemic distinctness (against which he adduces homonyms). But it would go ill with Chomsky's argument against any sane defender of the 'criterion', since the case against (i) or against (ii) might hold, but just what could not plausibly hold is the simultaneous case against both. To adopt Chomsky's language, the 'criterion' may perhaps be 'false in one direction': precisely what seems unlikely is that it could be shown to be, as Chomsky asserts, 'false in both directions'. This is because, as emerges from the following considerations, at least one part of Chomsky's dual case must be abandoned.

Before any substantive point could be debated between Chomsky and his opponent, they would have to agree on the question: 'Are we concerned with difference of meaning of tokens *in identical contexts,* or with difference of meaning of tokens *irrespective of context?*' The answer must be that they are concerned with difference of meaning of tokens in identical contexts, since if context is disregarded questions about token-meanings become conflated with questions about type-meanings. The distinction is no longer viable.[1]

Now if context is to be taken into account, the defender of the 'criterion' can claim that the argument from homonymy collapses straight away (since 'I saw him by the bank' i.e. river bank, and 'I saw him by the bank' i.e. First National, patently occur in different contexts: or, should they occur in identical contexts, then the token-meanings do not differ). It is pointless to invoke here the semantic difference 'bank (finance)' vs. 'bank (river)', since to apply that distinction to tokens in identical contexts is to impose a type-meaning classification, when what is at issue is a token-meaning difference. If, however, someone were to insist that homonyms are nonetheless token-meaning-different in identical contexts, the defender of the 'criterion' would then be justified in maintaining the counterclaim that *any* expressions are token-meaning-different in identical contexts (including synonyms). He does not have to be able to show what the difference is in order to substantiate such a claim: for that cannot be shown either in the case of homonymous tokens in identical contexts.

---

[1] If, for example, we have only a fragment of undated manuscript bearing just the words *milites moriuntur,* we are simply not in any position to contrast the token-meaning of these words with the type-meaning of the Latin words *milites moriuntur,* since the context is unknown. A similar position is reached by disregarding known contexts.

In short, the argument from homonymy can be pressed, ultimately, only at the expense of sabotaging the argument from synonymy. Likewise, if the argument from synonymy is maintained (by showing lack of token-meaning-difference between items in identical contexts), the argument from homonymy must be abandoned (since there will be parallel lack of token-meaning-difference between items in identical contexts).

Chomsky's best move here would be to press the argument from synonymy and drop the argument from homonymy. This means attacking the 'criterion' as a necessary condition of phonemic distinctness, at the expense of conceding it to provide a sufficient condition. But, for reasons to be examined below, it is precisely the 'criterion' as a necessary condition which is the least indispensable part of any case for a semantically based phonology. Indeed, it was a misrepresentation to contend that it constituted part of that case in the first place.

A further comment must be added concerning the question of equivalence (c), i.e. type-meaning equivalence. Here three points should be noticed. First, it is incorrect to claim, as Chomsky does, that the 'synonymity criterion' is properly applicable only to tokens. The phonologist who inquires, for example, whether [pil] and [bil] are phonemically distinct in English is not primarily concerned with tokens—that is, with single particular instances of these utterances— but rather with a general question of classification. He begs no questions by distinguishing between a type [pil] and a type [bil], since the types in question are phonetic types. And, in general, one may legitimately define an utterance-type in purely phonetic terms without in any way prejudging the question of its phonological status.[1] Second, if the 'synonymity criterion' is interpreted in this sense, i.e. as a thesis about phonetically defined utterance-types, it becomes irrelevant to cite cases of honomymy as weighing against it (since it will not prove possible to assign different meanings to distinct phonetic types of a given homonym.) Thirdly, granted this

[1] Various phonetic but non-phonological typologies for utterances might be suggested: cf. Rosetti 1963. In general, the type-token distinction may be set up in various ways with respect to any particular item. This point may perhaps best be illustrated by analogy. E.g. an English shilling may be regarded as a token of two or more coin-types, according to our interest in coin classification. It may or may not be relevant that it is made of silver alloy, or bears a certain monarch's head, or is valuable by reason of the small number of shillings minted in its particular year. Thus it may be regarded as a token of the type 'English silver shilling', or of the type 'George V shilling', or of the type '1930 shilling'. All the relevant characteristics are manifested *in praesentia* in the token.

interpretation, the 'synonymity criterion' does not in fact represent the position for which advocates of a semantically based phonology have usually argued or need argue.

Specifically, it is not usually argued that a phonemic distinction *must* differentiate meanings (of phonetically defined utterance types) but that such a distinction *may* differentiate meanings and (sometimes) *does* so in the language under investigation.[1] To bring up such examples as English *economics, adult,* etc. is thus to miss the point, since a semantically based phonological analysis of English will have no difficulty in establishing that in (many) other instances, the phonetic differences in question *do* distinguish meanings, and hence a correct phonological analysis of these differences will result.

A semantically based phonology is compatible with the denial of synonymy, provided phonological units can be established without exclusive reliance on controversial cases. The Bloomfieldian position[2] with regard to such pairs as /ekinámiks/ and /iykinámiks/ may be represented as follows: 'I assume that the two differ in meaning, although I am unable to ascertain what the difference is.' This may be an unprofitable assumption for purposes of semantic analysis; but that is not the question here. The issue between a Bloomfieldian phonologist and Chomsky must be whether or not such an assumption is consonant with a correct phonological analysis of English. If indeed all the pairs exhibiting the same phonetic differences as [ekinámiks] and [iykinámiks] were controversial cases, in the sense that no semantic distinction between the members of such pairs could be clearly established, a Bloomfieldian phonologist would have no ground for recognizing the distinction as phonological. But he is not committed to the proposition that failure to discover a semantic

---

[1] Fischer-Jørgensen 1956, p. 144: 'it is only required that a replacement should be *capable* of entailing a difference in the content, not that it should *always* do so.' Chomsky's formulation of the 'synonymity criterion' makes the error of representing the condition of meaning-difference as a necessary condition as well as a sufficient condition. Chomsky is not the only opponent of semantically based phonology guilty of this misrepresentation. Cf. Bloch 1948 32.2: 'It is customary to base the difference between distinctive and non-distinctive sounds on meaning: to say, for instance that any interchange of distinctive sounds will affect the meaning of a word or phrase, while any interchange of non-distinctive sounds will leave the meaning unaffected.' It is ironical that Bloch should refer for confirmation of this statement to Bloch and Trager 1942 3.1, where, however, the promised confirmation is not forthcoming. The position stated in Bloch and Trager 1942 3.1 coincides in fact with that of Fischer-Jørgensen (above): distinctive differences or contrasts are there said to be 'capable of distinguishing one meaning from another', but there is no claim that they must invariably do so. Cf. also Jones 1962 § 53: 'The sounds of separate phonemes do not *necessarily* distinguish words, but they are capable of doing so, and generally do so.'   [2] Cf. pp. 6–7.

difference in *one* such case is sufficient to justify classing the members of that pair as phonemically identical. Furthermore, for the Bloomfieldian it is only on condition that a semantic difference *can* be established for at least one such case that any question of assuming that /ekɨnámiks/ and /iykɨnámiks/ differ in meaning arises.

Finally, the theoretical obscurity of Chomsky's own position must be noted. It is far from clear why anyone should regard the 'pair test' in the form described by Chomsky as a test of phonemic distinctness, when what it is is manifestly something quite different, namely a test of auditory distinguishability of utterances. Such a test would, of course, become a test of phonemic distinctness if we had some guarantee that the utterance-tokens in question were not distinguishable by any other than phonemically relevant features. But any such proviso must of necessity involve the phonologist in circularity.

Nor can this circularity be broken by the proposal to define the phoneme simply by reference to the 'pair test': e.g. by saying 'Let us mean by *phonemically distinct* nothing more than *distinct as measured by the pair test*.' For the effect of such a proposal would be simply to equate 'phonological unit' with 'auditorily distinguishable unit', and for purposes of phonological analysis this equation is clearly intolerable.

It should be noted that this objection to the pair test is not to be confused with the objection that semantic knowledge may prompt the informant's replies. Critics of nonsemantically based phonology have sometimes failed to distinguish clearly between the two. Kohler, for example, speaks of 'the difficulty of knowing what sort of difference or identity the informant bases his judgement on, what constitutes difference or identity for him. He may react to English *burned* and *burnt* in the same way or differently according to whether he goes by sound or meaning, and it will be extremely difficult to devise tests that make it clear in each case which prompted him. Similarly, a German informant may classify utterances of the word *Regen* with uvular fricatives or lingual rolls as either different or the same. There is no way of separating this non-phonemic contrast from the phonemic one in the first example simply by taking note of the intuitive disposition of the informant. Not even the paired utterance test (Harris 1951 § 4.23) will be of any help in this case.'[1] This is true, but perhaps misleading. The pair test is inadequate,

[1] Kohler 1970, p. 301.

but not because it cannot be made proof against incorrect results arising from the fact that the informant may or may not use semantic criteria in classifying items as 'the same' or 'different'. The pair test cannot do the job required *even if* an assurance is available that the informant bases his replies on the sound and not the meaning of the test items.

The investigator concerned with analysing the role of systematic sound distinctions in the speech of a community must consider the various possible types or dimensions of communicational relevance which such distinctions may have. There is on this point a divergence of opinion among phonologists as to the scope of phonology.

The fact that in any given language certain utterances do and others do not have the same meaning is fundamental to the distinction between phonology and phonetics as drawn by Trubetzkoy. 'Die Phonologie hat zu untersuchen, welche Lautunterschiede in der betreffenden Sprache mit Bedeutungsunterschieden verbunden sind, wie sich die Unterscheidungselemente (oder Male) zueinander verhalten und nach welchen Regeln sie miteinander zu Wörtern (bezw. Sätzen) kombiniert werden dürfen.'[1] A characteristic feature of phonetics is its lack of concern with meanings: 'Besonders kennzeichnend für die Phonetik ist die vollkommene Ausschaltung jeder Beziehung zur sprachlichen Bedeutung der untersuchten Lautkomplexe.'[2] Whereas the basis of phonological description is the discovery that certain phonetic contrasts differentiate meanings. 'Der Anfang jeder phonologischen Beschreibung besteht in der Aufdeckung der in der betreffenden Sprache bestehenden bedeutungsdifferenzierenden Schallgegensätze.'[3] The notion 'capacity to differentiate meanings' thus enters into the definition of certain basic phonological concepts in Trubetzkoy's theory, notably that of 'phonological opposition' ('phonologische Opposition"), which Trubetzkoy introduces as follows: 'Schallgegensätze, die in der betreffenden Sprache die intellektuelle Bedeutung zweier Wörter differenzieren können, nennen wir phonologische (oder phonologisch distinktive oder auch distinktive) Oppositionen.'[4] The same applies to Trubetzkoy's concept of the phoneme, which is derived from that of phonological opposition, via that of 'phonological unit'. 'Unter

---

[1] Trubetzkoy 1939, p. 14.   [2] Trubetzkoy 1939, p. 13.
[3] Trubetzkoy 1939, p. 17.   [4] Trubetzkoy 1939, p. 30.

(direkt oder indirekt)[1] phonologischer Opposition verstehen wir also jeden Schallgegensatz, der in der gegebenen Sprache eine intellektuelle Bedeutung differenzieren kann. Jedes Glied einer solchen Opposition nennen wir phonologische (bezw. distinktive) Einheit.'[2] 'Phonologische Einheiten, die sich vom Standpunkt der betreffenden Sprache nicht in noch kürzere aufeinanderfolgende phonologische Einheiten zerlegen lassen, nennen wir Phoneme.'[3] The phoneme is thus essentially a meaning-distinguishing unit.[4]

If, then, a language has a given distinction D and a set of pairs a_1 vs. b_1, a_2 vs. b_2, a_3 vs. b_3 . . . such that both members of each pair are realizations of meaningful expressions, and each pair is differentiated solely by the distinction D (as e.g. English [p^{h}in] vs. [bin], [p^{h}i:k] vs. [bi:k], [p^{h}æt] vs. [bæt] . . . where D=[p^h] vs. [b]), it follows from the definitions cited above that D will constitute a phonological opposition if and only if for at least one pair a vs. b the expressions realized by a and b differ in meaning. For if this is not the case then D cannot be held to differentiate meanings. But since a and b cannot differ in meaning if they are realizations of synonymous expressions, it is a necessary condition that the expressions realized by some pair a and b should not be synonymous. Strictly, since the meanings Trubetzkoy specifies are 'intellectual meanings' (*intellektuelle Bedeutung*) the relationship in question between the expressions realized by a and b will be that of 'intellectual synonymy'. Thus, for every case in which D has the status of a phonological opposition, there must be at least one pair a and b which do not realize 'intellectually synonymous' expressions (although there may be other pairs in the same set which do). For every case in which D does not have the status of a phonological opposition, no pair in the set will realize 'intellectually synonymous' expressions. Thus determining the phonological status of D is tantamount to determining whether or not the relationship of 'intellectual synonymy' holds between expressions realized by the members of some pair a and b in the set.

The significance of the term 'intellectual meaning' derives from Trubetzkoy's acceptance of a distinction between phonology and

---

[1] The distinction between direct and indirect phonological oppositions is that the terms of indirect oppositions occur in complementary distribution but share no common phonetic features distinguishing them in the sound system of the language, whereas the terms of direct oppositions are not in complementary distribution (Trubetzkoy 1939, p. 32).

[2] Trubetzkoy 1939, pp. 32–33. [3] Trubetzkoy 1939, p. 34.

[4] The credit for being the first to advance this concept of the phoneme is given by Trubetzkoy to L. V. Ščerba (Trubetzkoy 1939, p. 34, n. 1).

phonostylistics, based on Bühler's analysis of the three functions of speech.[1] Phonology, in Trubetzkoy's view, is concerned only with the 'intellectual meanings' of expressions, that is to say with the 'representative' function of speech. All phonetic distinctions which serve the 'expressive' and 'appellative' functions are the concern of phonostylistics, not phonology. Thus from the phonological point of view any two expressions a and b may be considered synonymous if they differ in respect of the expressive or appellative functions, provided that they do not differ in respect of the representative function (whatever that is taken to be in a given case). E.g. if it is agreed that a and b have different meanings, but that the difference of meaning consists solely in that a expresses emotional involvement on the part of the speaker, whereas b is emotionally 'neutral' (cf. French [e'ppuvãtabl] vs. [epuvã'tabl]), this difference of meaning does not count against the assessment of a and b as 'intellectual synonyms'.

The importance of the function of distinguishing between 'intellectual meanings' is further evident in the rules given by Trubetzkoy for the determination of phonemes. The first rule is as follows: 'Wenn zwei Laute derselben Sprache genau in derselben lautlichen Umgebung vorkommen und mit einander vertauscht werden dürfen, ohne dabei einen Unterschied in der intellektuellen Wortbedeutung hervorzurufen, so sind diese zwei Laute nur fakultative phonetische Varianten eines einzigen Phonems.'[2] This rule is a statement of a sufficient condition for classifying the distinction between sound a and sound b as non-phonemic. By implication it states also a sufficient condition for refusing to classify two phonetically distinct meaningful items as realizations of synonymous expressions (i.e. if the two items differ solely in respect of sounds which always occur in the same environments and may always be interchanged without altering the 'intellectual meanings' in question, then the two items are formally (phonologically) identical, and hence there is no question of synonymity.)

Trubetzkoy does not always, however, take the existence of synonyms sufficiently into account, as in the formulation of the following rule: 'Wenn zwei Laute genau in derselben Lautstellung vorkommen und nicht mit einander vertauscht werden können, ohne dass sich dabei die Bedeutung der Wörter verändern oder das Wort unkenntlich werden würde, so sind diese zwei Laute phonet-

---

[1] Trubetzkoy 1939, pp. 17–29.
[2] Trubetzkoy 1939, p. 42.

ische Realisationen zweier verschiedener Phoneme.'[1] This rule states a sufficient condition for classifying the distinction between sound *a* and sound *b* as phonemic. But it falls foul of cases of the following kind. Suppose we are investigating the [t]/[d] distinction in a language in which all words are monosyllabics having the structure CV. We find that for some values of V there corresponds to [tV] a word pronounced [dV] with a different 'intellectual meaning'. In other cases there corresponds to [tV] no word *[dV]. But in a third class of cases there corresponds to [tV] a synonym pronounced [dV]. Under Trubetzkoy's rule cited above, the [t]/[d] distinction fails in this language to satisfy the sufficient condition for classification as a phonemic opposition. Yet, *ex hypothesi*, it is a distinction capable of distinguishing between 'intellectual meanings'. It must be assumed that Trubetzkoy either overlooked the possibility of such cases in formulating his rule, or else believed that they never occurred. To take such cases into account, the rule would need to be amended by adding some such proviso as 'or substitute for one word its intellectual synonym.'

The scope of phonology according to Trubetzkoy is more restricted than in the view of those linguists (e.g. Bloomfield) who draw no distinction between phonology and phonostylistics. The distinction between phonology and phonetics, on the other hand, is drawn very similarly in both cases. According to Bloomfield: 'The study of language can be conducted without special assumptions only so long as we pay no attention to the meaning of what is spoken. This phase of language study is known as *phonetics*[2]. . . . The study of *significant* speech-sounds is *phonology* or *practical phonetics*. Phonology involves the consideration of meanings.[3]' Like Trubetzkoy, Bloomfield distinguishes between distinctive and non-distinctive sound-features, and assigns the study of the former to phonology: 'The features of sound in any utterance, as they might be recorded in the laboratory, are the *gross acoustic features* of this utterance. Part of the gross acoustic features are indifferent (*non-distinctive*), and only a part are connected with meanings and essential to communication (*distinctive*).'[4]

Bloomfield further states: 'It is important to remember that practical phonetics and phonology presuppose a knowledge of meanings: without this knowledge we could not ascertain the

---

[1] Trubetzkoy 1939, p. 44.   [2] Bloomfield 1935, p. 75.
[3] Bloomfield 1935, p. 78.   [4] Bloomfield 1935, p. 77.

phonemic features.'[1] But the meanings relevant to a Bloomfieldian
analysis are not the 'intellectual meanings' of Trubetzkoy. Bloomfield's definition of meaning is a very broad one: 'the *meaning* of a
linguistic form (is) the situation in which the speaker utters it and the
response which it calls forth in the hearer.'[2] Bloomfield further
specifies that 'a very important part of every situation is the state of
the speaker's body' which includes 'the predisposition of his nervous
system, which results from all his experiences, linguistic and other.'[3]
It appears from this that the meaning of an expression for Bloomfield
encompasses both what Trubetzkoy terms its 'intellectual meaning'
and also elements which belong to the 'expressive' and 'appellative'
functions of speech. While admitting the difficulty of obtaining
reliable data about meanings,[4] Bloomfield nonetheless insists on the
importance of information about meanings as a prerequisite of
phonological analysis. 'Since we can recognize the distinctive
features of an utterance only when we know the meaning, we cannot
identify them on the plane of pure phonetics.'[5] 'The observer who
hears a strange language, notices those of the gross acoustic features
which represent phonemes in his own language or in other languages
he has studied, but he has no way of knowing whether these features
are significant in the language he is observing.'[6] However, it is not
necessary to start with a comprehensive account of the meaning of
every utterance under investigation: what is needed to discover the
phonemic distinctions is sufficient information to determine 'which
utterances are alike in meaning, and which are different.'[7]

Thus Bloomfield places the phonologist in essentially the same
position as Trubetzkoy: he is given sets of pairs of phonetically
different items and must determine which pairs are realizations of
expressions differing in meaning, and which are not. Since, however,
Bloomfield explicitly rejects the view that natural languages have
synonyms as untenable for purposes of linguistic analysis,[8] it follows
that the phonologist's task is to assign phonetically different pairs to
one or other of two classes; namely, pairs which are and pairs which
are not variant realizations of one and the same phonological form.
But Bloomfield's broader view of the scope of phonology means that
it will be sufficient for the phonologist to discover *any* consistent
difference between the situations in which members of a given pair

[1] Bloomfield 1935, pp. 137–138.   [2] Bloomfield 1935, p. 139.
[3] Bloomfield 1935, p. 141.   [4] Bloomfield 1935, pp. 139–142.
[5] Bloomfield 1935, p. 77.   [6] Bloomfield 1935, p. 93.
[7] Bloomfield 1935, p. 93.   [8] Bloomfield 1935, p. 145. Cf. pp. 6–7.

are uttered in order to claim that there is a difference of meaning and thus of (phonological) form. On this view, if it can be established that French [epuvã'tabl] is emotionally 'neutral' whereas [e'ppuvãt-abl] is emotionally 'committed', then /epuvã'tabl/ and /e'ppuvãtabl/ are different nonsynonymous expressions.

We thus encounter somewhat varying criteria for synonymy. According to one view, it is possible that two phonetically different types may be realizations of different synonymous expressions, although conveying different 'phonostylistic' information. According to another view, any systematic correlation between two different phonetic types and two different situational features or sets of features counts against the classification of those types as realizations of different synonymous expressions. And 'in between' these views one can envisage others, the criteria for synonymy varying according as the scope of phonology tends to be 'restricted' (Trubetzkoyan) or 'unrestricted' (Bloomfieldian). We may speak, then, of synonymy as related to the assumed scope of phonological investigations in any given case. Accordingly, the statement that a and b are synonymous may or may not imply the absence of distinctions of an expressive or appellative nature. In every case, however, the phonologist's concern with meanings ends with his postulating a sameness or difference of meaning between certain expressions. He is not further concerned with any 'positive' characterization of the meaning(s) in question, nor with justifying his postulation other than by reference to the analytic procedures which, qua phonologist, he employs. Such procedures must now be considered in some detail, since upon the nature of the procedures depends the question whether a clear operational criterion for synonymity can be given, or whether the semantically based phonologist is reduced to borrowing (with or without acknowledgement) from some (specified or unspecified) prior semantic theory.

It must first be noted that the claim that phonemic distinctions, by definition, distinguish meanings does not commit the claimant to the view that establishing a phonemic distinction between a and b is dependent on the prior discovery of a difference in meaning between a and b. This latter view has, however, been independently maintained. A well known article by Pike contends that ascertainment of certain semantic information is essential for the determination of phonemes:

'The phonemic analysis cannot be completed until some initial grammatical steps are taken. Perhaps the most important of these is the identification of at least a limited number of morphemes. Thus Hockett, and Bloch and Trager utilize pairs of utterances which (1) have different meanings, and (2) are minimally different in their pronunciation.

'Recognizing that the utterances are different in meaning is a grammatical process, not a phonemic one. It is thus absolutely essential that a minimal grammatical identification be achieved before phonemic analysis can be carried on: the irreducible minimum prerequisite is that the investigator know enough about two items to be sure that they are "different".'[1]

But if we must discover differences in meaning before we can establish phonemic distinctness, then since we cannot discover differences in meaning if we do not know what differences in meaning are, phonology becomes dependent upon a prior theory of meaning, or at least upon the prior acceptance of some partial theory of meaning— that part which deals with differences of meaning and thus with non-synonyms. But since synonymy and nonsynyonymy are heads and tails of the same coin, a theory of synonymy then becomes a pre-requisite of phonological analysis.

Some critics[2] of semantically based phonology evidently believe that appeal to meanings in phonological definitions and analytical procedures renders this conclusion inevitable, and, seeing no well established prior theory of synonymy available, reject semantically based phonology for this reason. Nor are matters improved by the fact that some semantically based phonologists commit the theoretical error of equating the discovery of differences in meaning with the discovery of informants' beliefs about differences in meaning. Or, if not equating the two, they are at least content to treat the former as directly derivable from the latter. Thus, for example, Fischer-Jørgensen contends that the necessary information can be obtained by the phonologist by 'eliciting short utterances and presenting them to a native who has to decide whether their meaning is the same or different'.[3] Specifically, the native speaker merely has to say 'yes' or 'no' to a direct question of the form 'Does *a* mean the same as *b*?' Fischer-Jørgensen goes to some lengths to justify this procedure and to explain why a simple 'yes/no' answer is adequate. The reason is

---

[1] Pike 1947, p. 158   [2] E.g. Chomsky. Cf. above.
[3] Fischer-Jørgensen 1956, p. 142.

that in the direct question 'the utterances are taken out of their natural (linguistic and non-linguistic) context. Consequently, these utterances have no contextual differences of meaning, and the native will react to them as representatives of classes of utterances and will react to their meanings as being the same (in the sense of representatives of one class of meaning) or different (in the sense of representatives of different classes of meaning). In most cases it is possible to leave this decision of being the same or different to the informant, simply because the relation between sound and meaning in the linguistic sign is arbitrary and unsystematic, so that it is rare that small differences of sound (which will be the crucial ones for the investigator) correspond to small and dubious differences of meaning, whereas it will normally happen that they correspond to obvious differences of meaning. . . .'[1] It appears from this that the linguist, in Fischer-Jørgensen's view, is engaged in the enterprise of discovering the proclaimed semantic beliefs[2] of speakers, in order to differentiate thereby phonemically distinct from non-phonemically distinct utterances. This is confirmed by the following revealing comment: 'Of course, if the linguist himself masters the language, the problem of avoiding meaning analysis is of no practical importance.'[3]

The implication is, clearly, that if the linguist speaks the language himself, then simple introspection will tell him which utterances differ in meaning and which do not. In other cases, where informants can be interrogated, it would seem that semantic distinctness—and hence phonemic distinctness—is established directly by informants' responses to questions about sameness of meaning.

Such a view is unacceptable as a basis for phonology, for at least two reasons. First of all, phonology cannot, any more than any other branch of linguistics, afford to ignore the distinction between fact and belief. Just as in grammar a distinction must be drawn between grammatical sentences and sentences which informants are willing to call 'grammatical', so here there must be no confusion between a difference of meaning and what informants are willing to call a 'difference of meaning'. Equally, in the case where the linguist is his

---

[1] Fischer-Jørgensen 1956, p. 142. Fischer-Jørgensen concedes that there may be borderline cases 'where gradual differences of sound will correspond to gradual differences of meaning'.

[2] Examples of statements which proclaim semantic beliefs are: (i) 'To disembark' means 'to go on shore from a ship', (ii) 'Rejection' does not mean the same as 'refusal', (iii) There is no French word which means the same as 'chair', (iv) 'Slithy toves' doesn't mean anything in English.

[3] Fischer-Jørgensen 1956, p. 142.

D

own informant, there must be no equating the ascertainment of semantic facts with introspection. By introspection, the linguist merely substitutes his own semantic beliefs for those of an informant —and this will not do, if linguistic analysis is to be counted as different from autobiography.

Second, even if semantic beliefs as proclaimed by speakers were held to reflect certain facts about meaning in a reliable way,[1] it is clear that the naïve pre-theoretical concept of 'meaning' appealed to in the question 'Does *a* mean the same as *b*?'—as put to an unsophisticated informant—is simply not the concept of meaning in which the linguist is interested (any more than the naïve pre-theoretical concept of a 'sound' corresponds to the linguist's 'phoneme': one might as well go about phonological analysis by asking informants directly 'Would you say these sounds are the same?'). But since, into the bargain, we have no guarantee that semantic beliefs—either in general or in particular instances—are based upon some uniform concept of meaning which language-users happen to have, exactly what it is that has been established when informants agree verbally upon (or when the linguist is himself introspectively sure of) a 'difference of meaning' is itself obscure. Nor can it be argued that least the linguist's own introspections are exempt from this obscurity. For to the extent that he is able to give some account of what it means to assert or deny sameness of meaning he is acting as his own analyst, not his own informant. The fact that the semantic beliefs under analysis are his own becomes at that point irrelevant.

The attempt to base phonological analysis upon direct establishment of the proclaimed semantic beliefs of native speakers destroys a parallelism which it is important to preserve between that side of the analysis which deals with sounds and that side which deals with meanings. The semantically based phonologist should start on the one hand from certain observable phonetic differences, and on the other from certain observable differences of usage. It will be his ultimate objective to determine how these may best be accounted for (i) by postulating phonemic differences, and (ii) by postulating differences in meaning. But are these two objectives attainable independently? If (i) is regarded as attainable independently of (ii), then the case for a semantically based phonology collapses. If (ii) is regarded as attainable independently of (i), it becomes incumbent

---

[1] This, of course, could never be established if we refused to make the distinction between semantic facts and semantic beliefs in the first place.

upon the theoretician of a semantically based phonology to set out and justify the semantic theory which guarantees his procedures and conclusions under (ii). But in fact he usually omits to do this,[1] starting his discussion at a point where it is assumed that one already has a fund of semantic information available.[2]

There is, however, a third possibility, which allows the inter-dependent attainment of both objectives. The account which follows argues that this third possibility provides a set of procedures which begs none of those questions which are indeed begged if we suppose that the phonologist has some separately acquired fund of semantic information. This argument, if successful, affords the phonologist a stance which is not vulnerable to the objections previously discussed. It will also be argued that one can arrive in this way at a criterion of synonymity which is adequate in the context of phonological analysis but which is not derived from a prior theory of the meanings of linguistic expressions.

Let the phonologist begin by establishing that there is a difference of usage[3] between a phonetic type a and some grossly dissimilar phonetic type b. This difference of usage is established without prejudice to the question whether it will ultimately be accounted for

---

[1] Trubetzkoy is a notable example. Another is Twaddell, who attempts to bypass the problem as follows: 'The events which correspond to the "same" form are phonetically significantly alike, for by "significant" we indicate the correlation of an utterance to a social situation. The phonetic events "Light the lamp" as produced by two different individuals are objectively very different; in so far as these events evoke similar responses in similar social situations, the two events are phonetically significantly alike.' (Twaddell 1935, p. 41.)

But taken literally this position allows for indefinitely many degrees of phonemic distinctness, since different events, different social situations and different responses will always be similar up to a point, but up to a different point in different cases. To say that the phonologist recognizes formal identity 'in so far as' events have certain similarities dispenses from the obligation to specify the semantic conditions further; but 'in so far as' wins this dispensation at the cost of opening a Pandora's box full of disparate similarities.

[2] It is undoubtedly this, in part at least, which has led Chomsky and others to view semantically based phonology with scepticism. One cannot take seriously a claim to the effect that phonemes distinguish meanings, when it rests merely upon a procedural assumption which no-one ever justifies.

[3] A difference of usage is established by finding correlations of the following kind which hold for all the data under observation. Let ap be the proposition that for all the a-tokens, an a-token occurs only if p, and pa the proposition that if p then no a-token occurs. Similarly for b and q the propositions bq and qb. For a, b p, and q together, we have eight such propositions: ap, pa, aq, qa, bp, pb, bq and qb. Then a difference of usage between the phonetic types a and b is defined as any difference which can be stated in a conjunction of the following form: $ap. bq. qa. pb$. Since the satisfaction of such a conjunction depends simply on establishing the truth values for the component propositions, we in no way prejudge the question whether items for which a difference of usage is established are realizations of expressions having the same meaning or different meanings.

in terms of a difference in meaning. For example, if the phonologist's informants are willing to apply a-tokens to members of a certain class of objects a but reject their application to members of a disjoint class of objects β, but, conversely, apply b-tokens to objects of class β, while rejecting their application to members of class a, such tests could reasonably be taken as establishing a difference of usage between a and b. The phonologist may then bring forward a phonetic type b' having some minor point of phonetic difference with b, in order to determine whether or not b and b' are phonologically distinct. The tests with a-objects and β-objects may be repeated, substituting b' for b. If exactly the same results ensue,[1] the phonologist may then formulate a provisional hypothesis (H) as follows:

H 'Either (i) b and b' do not contrast phonologically, or (ii) b and b' differ in phonological form but are noncontrastive in the dimension of communicational relevance under investigation.'

The dimension of communicational relevance depends on the values of p and q, and on the range of speech situations tested. Reference has already been made earlier to such general dimensional distinctions as 'representative' vs. 'appellative' and 'representative' vs. 'expressive'[2]; but other distinctions may be envisaged.

The investigator must then test H by attempting to discover values of p and q lying within the appropriate dimension, for which the conjunction $bp.b'q.qb.pb'$ is satisfied. On failure to discover such values for p and q, H may be considered established.

The next step is to determine which of the alternatives H (i) or H (ii) is preferable. This may be done as follows. Let the phonetic difference between b and b' be called D. Further pairs of items (k-k', l-l'...), each pair differing solely by D, must be examined.[3] Each pair will be tested against other phonetic types (r, s...) when a difference of usage can be demonstrated between such a type and either member of the pair. These tests will show whether or not a hypothesis corresponding to H, within the appropriate dimension of communicational relevance, can be established for k and k'. By testing k-k', l-l'...the phonologist can establish a matrix of the values of D for a number of phonetic pairs. This matrix will show the regularity with which D is associated with differences of usage for various phonetic types in

---

[1] i.e. if $ap. bq. qa. pb. b'q. qb'$ with values of p and q held constant, allowing for the substitution of b' for b.

[2] It is by no means clear that these distinctions are entirely satisfactory.

[3] The problem of defining D is for present purposes irrelevant: i.e. whichever value(s) of D the phonologist decides to investigate, the procedures here described are valid.

the language.   Such a matrix must be interpreted by the phonologist in the light of the following two methodological principles:

1.   Any assignment of phonological status which has the effect of proliferating pairs which differ in form but are noncontrastive in the dimension of communicational relevance is suspect.

2.   Any such assignment which creates a substantial class of pairs which fall under a general rule of form F, where F is 'For every phonetic type having the phonological characteristic(s) M there is a paired type having the phonological characteristic(s) N' must be rejected.

These two principles, which embody the phonologist's version of Occam's razor, ensure that the phonological status of D will be decided in such a way as to comply with the rejection of H(ii), I(ii), J(ii)...wherever possible.

Two general conditions must also be stipulated concerning the differences of usage upon which matrices are based.

The first condition is that the differences of usage which the phonologist establishes in investigating the phonological status of a given phonetic difference or set of differences must show 'dimensional similarity'.   This condition is simply a safeguard against conflating in one and the same analysis facts which properly belong to separate analyses.   The condition would be infringed, for example, if the phonologist admitted simultaneously as evidence bearing on the phonological status of one distinction both (i) a difference in usage between a and b which consisted in their use by speakers of different regional provenance and (ii) a difference in usage between c and d which consisted in their application by speakers of whatever regional provenance to different objects.   Two such differences show too great a dimensional dissimilarity to be reliably included in the same analysis.[1]

The second condition is that the differences of usage must be 'informational': i.e. we assume that no conventional[2] correlation

---

[1] It is easy to exemplify relatively gross infringements of the condition; but no detailed dimensional theory of usage seems to have been worked out by linguists. Conceivably, there might be relevant phonological differences within the 'representative' function of speech which Trubetzkoy correlates with the province of phonology: e.g. there might be, to adopt Malinowski's distinctions, a phonology of pragmatic utterances, a phonology of narrative, and a phonology of phatic communion—at least for certain languages. Similarly, there might be some point in distinguishing a phonology of statements, a phonology of questions, a phonology of exclamations, and so on. Such matters have not been at all fully explored.

[2] i.e. non-natural. Phonology has no concern with phonic differences attributable to natural causes (e.g. age, sex, physiognomy).

between phonetically differing items and different usages is the concern of the linguist unless there is evidence to show that speakers are aware of the correlation. This condition, in appearance trivial, is in fact not so, since it can be shown that some accounts of linguistic analysis, e.g. Bloomfield's, fail to satisfy it. It would, for example, be sufficient in principle for a Bloomfieldian linguist to establish any consistent correlation between two phonetically different items and two different situational features in order to conclude that the expressions in question differed in meaning. The difference in usage need not, in Bloomfield's formulation, be informational. But if speakers are unaware of the situational difference in question, no information about such a difference is conveyed by any linguistic forms they use. The reason for saying this is simply the common-sense reason that if we are prevented by ignorance from drawing even a hazardous inference from p to q, or the probability of q, then p can in no sense inform us that q. For example, for a strictly mono-gamous community unaware of the connexion between sexual intercourse and childbirth, it would be inaccurate to identify the informational difference between their use of the word for a woman's offspring and the word for a woman's male consort after the birth of an offspring with that between English *father* and *child*. The con-dition of 'informationality' stipulates that it would be irrelevant for the linguist to establish that the one word applied only to fathers and the other only to their children; since the community *ex hypothesi* lacks the relevant concepts, whatever informational difference there might be uses of the two words, it could not be, either in whole or in part, *that* difference. Likewise, if in a given language there is only one mid back vowel, and in the north it is real-ized as [o], whereas in the south it is realized as [ɔ], the correlation is 'informational' only if there is recognition of [o] as a 'northern' pronunciation and [ɔ] as a 'southern' pronunciation. For without such recognition, the difference in pronunciation between e.g. [pot] and [pɔt] cannot in the relevant sense give information about the speakers, i.e. information about their provenance: it thus fails to qualify as a conventional phonic difference relevant to the analysis of the expressive function of speech in that community.

The condition of 'informationality', it should be noted, is not based upon any specific view of the proper way to define the 'meaning' of an expression, but simply upon the point that a language is an instrument of communication and the epistemological principle that what is not known cannot be communicated.

The main point of the foregoing formulation of phonological methodology is to give full recognition to the fact that phonological differences are always, and necessarily, relative to some dimension or dimensions of communicational relevance. Once this is acknowledged, it is obvious in which respects the debate between critics and defenders of semantically based phonology was fundamentally misconceived. (What phonologists have commonly failed to do is to recognize—or, at least, to state explicitly—the communicationally relevant dimension taken as basic to their establishment of phonological units. But it is not difficult to see what in practice it usually turns out to be; namely, the function of phonetic types as realizations of expressions used to differentiate reference to objects and properties of objects in the physical world.[1] This is what underlies the view that the 'word' is the basic context for phonological analysis,[2] and also what in part accounts for the way in which stress and intonation features are often treated as addenda to more primitive segmental structures.[3]

We may now put in its proper perspective the question as to whether we are to subsume the whole range of dimensions of communicational relevance under the term 'meaning' as used in 'meaning of an expression'. This would certainly run counter to traditional

[1] This is explicitly acknowledged as an assumption made in phonological analysis by Kohler: 'words are first of all names for parts of the body, for tools, for properties of these, for numbers and for units which behave in the same way as these 'basic words', but cannot be divided into units that are again 'basic words' (Kohler 1970, p. 302).

[2] The extreme view on this point is represented by Daniel Jones, who restricts the application of the term 'phoneme' to occurrence within words. 'The restriction "in a word" is important. To extend the definition to cover word-groups or sentences would greatly complicate matters . . . it might even be found to render the elaboration of any consistent theory of phonemes impossible. . . .' (Jones 1962 § 34).

[3] It is sometimes presented in the guise of a psychological justification for treating some phonological distinctions as more fundamental than others. 'Since the differentiation of semantic units is the least dispensable among the sound functions in language, speech participants learn primarily to respond to the distinctive features. It would be deceptive, however, to believe that they are trained to ignore all the rest in speech sounds. Beside the distinctive features, there are, at the command of the speaker, also other types of coded information-bearing features that any member of a speech community has been trained to manipulate and which the science of language has no right to disregard.' (Jakobson and Halle 1956 § 2.3). These additional features include 'configurative features' which 'signal the division of the utterance into grammatical units of different degrees of complexity', and 'expressive features' which 'put the relative emphasis on different parts of the utterance or on different utterances and suggest the emotional attitudes of the utterer'. Whereas the more fundamental features, i.e. the distinctive features, are those capable of differentiating morphemes. It is hardly coincidental that the first explanatory illustration of the operation of distinctive features given in Jakobson and Halle should be that of the host at a party introducing his guests to one another by name (Jakobson and Halle 1956 § 1.1).

usage. For example, suppose the values of p and q in a certain phonological investigation are established in terms of the regional provenance of speakers (region A vs. region B), then the fact that two phonetic types emerged as 'phonologically distinct' although not differing in usage under the tests proposed would not normally be taken as counting towards establishing their synonymity.

In other words, the synonymy postulate may be regarded as one specific form of a more general postulate, namely

'There may be pairs of expressions of L which differ in form but not in some dimension(s) of communicational relevance.'

But let us now suppose that we have come to some decision about what dimensions of communicational relevance we wish to subsume under the term 'meaning'. We thereby propose a specific interpretation of the synonymy postulate, and may on the same basis, if we so wish, define the scope of a (semantically based) phonological investigation.

It may be observed in this connexion that the two methodological principles advanced above do all that is required of them. They are the principles which, once the application of the term 'meaning' is fixed in a certain way, give rise to such phonological concepts as 'free variation' and 'neutralization'.

There is in semantically based phonology a close connexion between these concepts and that of synonymy. 'Free variation' and 'neutralization' may both, from a certain viewpoint, be seen as safeguards against the proliferation of synonyms. For example, if a linguist investigates the hypothesis that a language has the phonemic oppositions /p/ vs. /b/, /t/ vs. /d/ and /k/ vs. /g/, and finds that as regards the /p/ vs. /b/ opposition (but not the other two) all pairs of items differentiated solely by that opposition show no difference of usage, this will be a reason in favour of modifying the hypothesis by treating [p] and [b] as free variants.[1] By this revision the provisional phoneme inventory is reduced by one, and the provisional lexicon is consequently alleviated by the removal of a set of potential synonym pairs involving simply the /p/ vs. /b/ distinction, each such pair being now replaceable by a single entry. Similarly, in such a language as Spanish we have the choice between accepting a great proliferation of synonym pairs of the type /ganar/ 'to gain': /ganaɾ/ 'to gain', and saying that the opposition /r/ vs. /ɾ/ is neutralized in final position.

---

[1]Assuming there are no features of the distribution of [p] and [b] which argue against their treatment as free variants.

The reason why it is preferable to accept the latter alternative is twofold. First, back door admissions make nonsense of front door refusals. By adhering rigorously to the principle 'once a phoneme always a phoneme' we would simply be achieving a certain 'front door' uniformity of phonological description at the expense of a very great 'back door' multiplication of lexical entries for Spanish. Second, the principle itself is brought in disrepute if the class of candidates admitted at the back door contains all and only those refused at the front. The possibility in this hypothetically expanded Spanish lexicon of subsuming the relevant synonym pairs under a general rule of form F (i.e. 'for every lexical entry ending in /-r/ there is a corresponding synonym ending in /-ɾ/') shows that we are dealing with a fact which should properly be accounted for at the level of phonology. In short, a semantically based phonology may be said to operate under the standing prohibition: *synonyma non multiplicanda praeter necessitatem*.

Two further comments on the second of the two principles are in point here. First, the provision 'a substantial class of pairs' takes care of the kind of objection raised by Ebeling to the employment of semantic criteria in determining phonological differences:

> 'Usually linguists refer in this connection to meaning. But this cannot be done consistently. An example may illustrate this: the Russian words *škaf* and *škap* are usually regarded as synonyms. If we base, however, our criterion for the distinction between relevant and nonrelevant differences of sound upon meaning, we must admit that in Russian immediately after *ška-* the opposition stop versus continuant is neutralized in contact with labiality and orality. Nevertheless, nobody seems to accept this formulation. To every Russian [škaf] and [škap] are no doubt two different forms. This criterion should prevail everywhere as it does in this case.
>
> 'I take an English example from Hockett: *root* may be pronounced [ruwt] or [rut]. In such cases the environment, *ška-* or *r-t*, is usually considered too complicated or too specific for the assumption of a neutralizing influence, but this can only mean that probably a native speaker will not be inclined to interpret the forms as the same: we can in no way dispense with an appeal to his interpretation.'[1]

Evidently, the exact number which counts as a 'substantial class' is open to argument; but it is nonetheless a different way of deciding

[1] Ebeling 1960, p. 38.

the issue from appealing to the native speaker's *Sprachgefühl*. To reject *škaf* and *škap* as an example of neutralization because it would be a unique example is in no sense equivalent to admitting *škaf* and *škap* as synonyms because that is how Russian speakers feel about the matter.

Second, there will doubtless be cases in which the admission of two sounds as contrasting phonologically creates a substantial class of synonym pairs, even though that solution is imposed by other examples in which a difference of usage within the same dimension of communicational relevance can be shown to depend solely on the distinction between the sounds in question. (Such cases may even be common in a language where the phonological system is undergoing a change at certain points.) It will be the duty of the phonologist to draw attention to such 'inconsistencies' in the way the language utilizes sound differences; but the validity of the principle invoked above is in no way called in question by these cases.

Subject to the interpretation already discussed, the phonologist's criterion of synonymity may be formulated as follows:

> 'Two phonetic types are realizations of synonymous expressions if they show no difference of usage and the phonetic difference between them is also that between other pairs of phonetic types which do show a difference of usage.'

This criterion goes no further than giving a sufficient condition for synonymous expressions, and this is adequate for purposes of phonological analysis, since the aim of the phonologist is here limited to discovering the phonological distinctions of *L*. To draw up a complete inventory of synonymous pairs for *L* lies outside his province qua phonologist. He is interested merely in such synonymous pairs as have phonetic realizations sufficiently alike to raise the question of whether or not he is dealing with phonologically identical items. These are the cases in which it may be in doubt whether it is correct to account for the facts of communication by setting up one expression, or two expressions differing in form but not in meaning.

Thus the essential feature of synonymity statements here is their role as providers of an alternative explanation of the fact that two phonetic types may have no discoverable difference of usage.

The role is a vital one because without this alternative the phonological analysis breaks down. If synonymity statements are eliminated the case of phonetic types not differing in usage can be dealt with in only one of two ways; either (i) by assigning the same phonological form to both members of the pair, irrespective of other pairs showing the same phonetic difference, or (ii) by treating the pair in question as realizations of expressions differing in both form and meaning. But (i) will lead to inconsistency in the phonological classification of the phonetic difference should there be other pairs where the same difference proves to be correlatable with a difference in usage, while accepting (ii) introduces the paradox of two expressions allegedly differing in both form and meaning but not differing in usage. To admit either possibility would be tantamount to admitting the inadequacy of the analytic procedures employed.

CHAPTER THREE

Synonymy and grammatical analysis

The availability of synonymity statements may be exploited in various ways in stating the grammar of a natural language. Here it is proposed to consider their role in connexion with morpheme variant (or allomorph) patterning, grammatical ambiguity, and transformational relations.

The question of morpheme variants raises a prior general issue: to what extent is 'sameness of meaning' relevant at all to morphological analysis? As in the case of phonological analysis, two views stand in conflict. On the one side it is maintained that morphological analysis requires semantic information about the data under analysis, and that semantic considerations enter into the definition of morphological units. Hence such definitions of the morpheme as 'a linguistic form which bears no partial phonetic-semantic resemblance to any other form',[1] or 'any form . . . which cannot be divided into smaller meaningful parts',[2] or 'the smallest individually meaningful elements in the utterances of a language'.[3] On the other side, it is maintained that criteria of form and distribution alone are adequate for morphological analysis, and so morphological units may be defined without reference to semantic considerations. Hence such assertions as 'distribution suffices to determine phonemes and morphemes and to state a grammar in terms of them',[4] or 'it would certainly not be impossible to determine roughly the morphemes of long enough printed texts without taking meaning into consideration'.[5]

Two questions concerning synonymy therefore arise: (i) is it possible to make good the claim, inherent in the procedures of non-semantically based morphology, that morphological analysis does not require a concept of synonymy? (ii) supposing this claim to be false or irrelevant, what then is the function of a concept of synonymy in relation to morphological analysis?

---

[1] Bloomfield 1935, p. 161.   [2] Bloch and Trager 1942, § 4.2.
[3] Hockett 1958, § 14.1.   [4] Harris 1954, § 5.   [5] Bazell 1954.

The answer to the first of these questions depends on how the scope of morphological analysis is envisaged. To avoid involvement with the varying interpretations of the terms 'morpheme', 'morph', 'allomorph' etc., we may call the units with which morphology deals 'M-units', and distinguish between various views of the scope of morphological analysis by reference to different concepts of such a unit.

If it is observed that in a language there are certain restrictions on the occurrence of phonemes or sequences of phonemes which cannot be brought within the scope of plausible phonological rules, and if it is desired to account for these restrictions in terms of units of a different order from the phoneme, such units (M-units) may be set up without appeal to meanings.[1] This assertion commits us to no assumption about concerning linguistic structure, however, for the question belongs to the empirical methodology of morphological analysis.

Clearly, the decision to set up M-units in a particular case will depend on the usefulness of so doing in order to account for certain facts of (non-phonologically determined) distribution. But these include facts of varying generality and different kinds of importance. It is therefore slightly beside the point to cite, as does Zellig Harris,[2] cases such as English *persist* and *person*, in an attempt to show the superiority of nonsemantically based morphology. Harris argues that 'if the morphemic composition of a word is not easily determined, we cannot decide the matter by seeing what are the component meanings of the word and assigning one morpheme to each. Do *persist*, *person* contain one morpheme each or two? In terms of meaning, it would be difficult to decide, and the decision would not necessarily fit into any resulting structure. In terms of distribution we have *consist*, *resist*, *pertain*, *contain*, *retain*, and the like (related in phonemic composition and in sentence environment), but no such set for *person*; hence we take *persist* as two morphemes, *person* as one.'

But all this example shows is that there is *a* nonsemantic criterion available which gives a certain solution. There is also, however, a semantic criterion available which gives a different solution (i.e.

---

[1] No need arises to offer an argument in support of this proposition. If the sequences governed by the restrictions are given as sequences of nonmeaningful units (phonemes), the problem is no different from that of stating macro-unit combinatorial rules for any set of nonlinguistic micro-unit sequences (e.g. the marks of a wallpaper pattern). Argument, on the other hand, would be required in support of the opposite view, namely the assumption that semantic information is necessary in order to do this.   [2] Harris 1954, § 4.

persist and *person* as single M-units on the ground that no cut yields independently meaningful segments). What needed demonstration to prove the point was not the availability of *some* nonsemantic (distributional) criterion, but either (a) the existence of a 'correct' answer to which the distributional criterion leads directly, but the semantic criterion dubiously, if at all, or (b) that the solution given by the distributional criterion is useful, whereas that given by the semantic criterion is not, or less so. But, as regards (a) it would clearly be question-begging to assume that the analysis *per-sist* is correct and *per-son* incorrect in order to show the improbability of producing a correct analysis by semantic criteria. As regards (b), no attempt at all is made to assess the utility of the preferred analysis, which in fact turns out to be of a somewhat low order. We can thereby it is true, subsume certain morphological facts about English verbs under a general rule (e.g. 'English verbs admit the structure AB but not BA where A=*'per-, re-, con-* . . .' and B=*'-sist, -tain* . . .'); but the same facts can be stated hardly less economically on the supposition that the forms are monomorphemic ('The class of English verbs includes *persist, resist, consist, pertain, retain, contain* . . but excludes **sistper, *sistre, *sistcon, *tainper, *tainre, *taincon.* . . .').[1]

Moreover, the facts in question are relatively unimportant in the sense that an infringement of the rule merely produces a non-English lexical item in an otherwise grammatical English arrangement (e.g. **The defenders did not sistre* for *The defenders did not resist*), which is tantamount to saying that no basic grammatical distinction of English would be obliterated if the language admitted both the permitted and the excluded sequences. Admission of the excluded sequence would merely require that the lexicon of English be expanded to accommodate such synonym pairs as *resist/sistre, contain/taincon* etc.[2]

On the other hand, if morphology is envisaged as extending to

[1] There is no comparison here with the situation which would arise if a criterion gave *he eats, they eat* etc. as monomorphemic, and a rule consequently had to exclude specifically by listing **he eat, *they eats* etc.

[2] Furthermore, the apparent determinacy of the nonsemantic solution in Harris's example is to some extent illusory. It is doubtless easy to find analogies which will support splitting *persist* into *per-sist*. Nonetheless, some can be found, if one looks hard enough, to support splitting *person* into *per-son* (e.g. *parson, mason, pervert, Persian*). What remains unanswered, if one relies on nonsemantic criteria, is the question how many supporting analogies have to be found, and how closely they have to conform to the distribution of the form under analysis. Any investigation of such questions is likely to reveal a continuous scale of 'phonetic-distributional likeness', which leaves the investigator—not the criterion—to decide when there is a 'sufficient likeness' to support one analysis rather than another.

include what may be called 'M-relations' (e.g. 'plural of', 'past tense of'), then it becomes questionable whether nonsemantic criteria can produce an adequate analysis. It would seem that the most powerful theory of M-relations achievable on the basis of nonsemantic criteria is one which would be incapable of explaining e.g. what is meant by describing *went* as the past tense of *go*.

The units between which M-relations hold are items which traditional grammar normally treats as different morphological forms of the same 'word', e.g. *look* and *looked*, *bonus* and *bonum*, *je* and *moi*, and it is relevant to observe that the metalanguage of traditional grammar acknowledges the distinction between M-relations and mere grammatical classification: e.g. one says that *looked* is the past tense of *look*, or that *bonum* is the neuter of *bonus*, or that *moi* is the strong form (disjunctive form) of *je*, whereas of *looked* and *see*, or of *bonum* and *clarus*, or of *moi* and *il*, one does not say that one is any kind of form of the other—instead, the similarities or differences in their grammatical behaviour are described by simple classification (e.g. by categorizing them as 'verb', 'past', 'adjective', 'neuter' etc.).[1]

But it is a nontrivial fact about natural languages that M-relations may obtain between items not identifiable by criteria of formal resemblance, and this fact precludes one possible basis for an account of M-relations which would exclude semantic considerations. This is perhaps best illustrated by means of a hypothetical example.

Suppose that *zoff* is an English verb occurring in such sentences as *I usually prefer to zoff it*, *They turn out better if you zoff them* etc., and the question arises how we may determine whether or not *zoffed* is the past tense of *zoff*. The claim that we may resolve this question by using exclusively nonsemantic criteria implies of course that we do not need to take into consideration the distribution of these items in semantically acceptable contexts, but simply their

---

[1] The term 'grammatical synonym' has been proposed by Winter for sets like English *walked*, *went* and *came*, and 'may be applied equally well to entire constructions and to fractions of constructions, whenever these can be isolated by strictly formal procedures' (Winter 1964, pp. 14–15). By this is meant that the forms 'are synonymous in respects other than lexical meaning'. This proposal, however, stands in need of considerable clarification, since according to Winter 'the basic characteristics of a set of synonyms are that they have a comparable range of distribution (or meaning)—they are synonymous only to the extent that they do just that ——'. It is not clear exactly how to take the 'or' here in 'distribution (or meaning)', and this is one reason why it is not clear whether e.g. pairs like *boy* and *girl* would count as 'grammatical synonyms'. Another reason is that unless some criterion is proposed for determining exactly what is included in 'lexical meaning', it is difficult to decide whether forms 'are synonymous in respects other than lexical meaning'.

distribution in the grammatical sentences of English. Now if *zoffed* is in fact the past tense of *zoff*, *zoffed* will occur in a set of environments in which it is substitutable *salva grammaticalitate* for such forms as *spliced, crossed, missed,* etc., which are not presumably correctly describable as 'past tense forms of *zoff*'. That is to say, granted distributional definitions of the notions 'past tense form' and 'present tense form' such that *zoff, splice,* etc. count as presents and *zoffed, spliced,* etc. as pasts, we are still left without a criterion to effect unique M-relation pairings between members of the two classes. Therefore, to be the past tense of *zoff* cannot be simply to be a member of a certain class of forms interchangeable *salva grammaticalitate*. But all that apparently remains to distinguish (nonsemantically) *zoffed* from *spliced, crossed, missed,* etc. in a way that clearly links *zoff* with *zoffed* and excludes the pairings *zoff—spliced* etc. is the formal (i.e. phonological) constitution of *zoffed*. If, however, this is the sole differentia which singles out *zoffed* as that member of the class of past tense forms which is the past tense of *zoff*, it becomes apparent that the notion 'past tense of' reduces to the conjunction of a distributional classification (i.e. 'past tense form') and a phonological classification (i.e. '/zof/+...').

The example may be taken as illustrating a general strategy for reducing any M-relation to concepts which remain within the limits of nonsemantically based morphology. But against anyone who is tempted to defend this reduction by maintaining that an M-relation *is* just the conjunction of a distributional and a phonological classification, two points must be made. First, that if so, then there are indefinitely many M-relations, most of which no-one would dream of calling a grammatical relation at all (e.g. that between an English noun and English adjective with a phonologically common segment: *dent, dental; gent, gentle; roof, rueful;* etc.)[1] Second, that in cases of the relationship between forms where the phonological resemblance involved is nil (as e.g. in saying that *went* is the past tense of *go*) there is no basis for identifying the invariant which is implied in the concept of an M-relation. For any useful concept of an M-relation must be essentially that of a two-place predicate M such that to

---

[1] If it is counterargued that reducing M-relations to distributional-cum-phonological classifications does not commit us to the view that *all* such classifications define M-relations, the question then arises how we know which classifications do and which do not, and to this there seems to be no answer which can be arrived at by invoking solely nonsemantic criteria. The reductionist cannot both have his bun and eat (part of) it.

assert $M(ab)$ implies the existence of some linguistic entity realized in common by a and by b. Pursuing the analysis further, it is evident that statements to the effect that b is the past tense of a have the underlying logical form:

$$\exists x \; (M_1 \; (ax).M_2(bx))$$

—that is to say, we assert that there is an entity x (in this case a verb) such that a is its infinitive form and b its past tense form. But it there were to be cases where phonological resemblance or lack of it between a and b just did not count, then the M-relation would amount simply (by the reductionist thesis) to a distributional classification. This means that the past tense of a in such a case must be reckoned to be any item which falls into the distributional class 'past tense form', and this consequence is clearly intolerable. E.g. if we suppose that *zoff* may have a past tense form phonologically unrelated to *zoff*, we are left with no plausible method of identifying the form in question among the members of the class of English past tense forms, whether or not that class includes *zoffed*.

Nor can this reductionist dilemma be avoided by treating such instances as deviations from a standard case in which both phonological and distributional criteria are involved, as e.g. to say that *went* is to *go* as *looked* is to *look*,[1] except that the phonological resemblance in the former case is nil. For if appeal to meanings is dispensed with, then *went* can no more be established as the past tense of *go* than as the past tense of any other verb lacking a phonologically 'regular' past tense form. (If there happens to be only one 'irregular' pair in the system, a simple process of elimination will ensure the correct pairing; but good luck should not be confused with adequacy of the criterion employed.) We cannot in any sense 'suspend' the requirement of phonological resemblance in order to link *went* with *go*, as we might e.g. suspend a colour-bar rule in order to let black Mrs. Smith accompany her white husband. Waiving a general rule in favour of a particular relationship assumes that the relationship is established—or in principle establishable—in advance of the rule. But this will not do where the purpose of the rule is precisely to establish such relationships.

Parallel arguments can be adduced for any M-relation. It must be concluded that a theory of M-relations which explicates them solely in terms of phonological-cum-distributional classification is ill

---

[1] The proportion is inexact in that *went* does not function as a part participle, as does *looked*; but this may be ignored for purposes of the example.

E

suited to the purposes of linguistic analysis, since it embraces on the one hand relations of no conceivable linguistic interest, while sometimes excluding on the other hand relations between items having functions exactly analogous to those between which M-relations hold. There is simply no point in having such a theory of M-relations to account for how natural languages work. For all it can do in the way of accounting for non-phonologically conditioned distribution patterns can already be done without reference to M-relations at all.[1] Whereas if we seek to account for the morphological phenomena of 'variable words' in general, we shall need a more powerful theory which covers both cases where there is and cases where there is not a parallelism between form and function.

A more radical reductionist thesis, avoiding appeal to phonological resemblance altogether, is embodied in the proposal that the morpheme, as distinct from the morph, be regarded as a factor of distributional proportion. Lyons argues in favour of this proposal as follows:

'To say that *worse* is composed of two morphemes, one of which it shares with *bad* (and *worst*) and the other of which it shares with *taller, bigger, nicer*, etc., is equivalent to saying that *worse* differs from *taller, bigger, nicer*, etc. in grammatical function (that is, in its distribution throughout the sentences of English) in the way that *bad* differs from *tall, big, nice*, etc. (and *worst* from *tallest*, etc.). This is commonly expressed as a proportion of grammatical, or distributional, equivalence. . . .

bad: *worse*: *worst*=*tall*: *taller*: *tallest*

This proportion expresses the fact that, for example, *worse* and *taller* (as well as *bigger, nicer*, etc.) are grammatically alike in that they are the comparative forms of the adjective—they can occur in such sentences as *John is worse (taller,* etc.*) than Michael, It is getting worse (taller,* etc.*) all the time. Worse* and *taller* (as well as *bigger, nicer*, etc.) differ from one another, however, in that they cannot occur in exactly the same set of sentences—for instance, as traditional grammarians would say, they cannot 'qualify' exactly the same set of nouns. In so far as the class of nouns which can be qualified by

---

[1] E.g. by recognizing as M-units such forms as *he, she, they*, and also *eat, eats, find, finds*, and formulating a selectional rule which forbids the combinations **he eat, *they eats*, etc., we can account for restrictions of great generality in English. But in order to do this we do not need to say e.g. that *they* is the plural of *he, she*, or that *eats* is the third person singular of *eat*; introducing M-relations adds nothing to the precision or generality of the selectional rule.

a particular adjective is grammatically determined . . . this feature of their distribution is accounted for by postulating a particular morpheme as a component of one adjective and another morpheme as a component of another adjective which 'qualifies' a different class of nouns.'[1]

Interpreted as a theory of M-relations, this means that a statement to the effect that the comparative of *bad* is *worse* (or '*bad*+-*er*→ *worse*') reduces to a distributional proportion *bad:worse=tall:taller* etc.[2]

The first point which calls for comment about this proposal is that, conspicuously, one of the environments in which *tall* occurs is the environment '...-*er*', and it is just the fact that *bad* does not occur in this environment which gives rise to the need for factorization. Thus it would seem that the proportion *bad:worse=tall:taller* cannot be an identical proportion (in spite of the sign '='), for it is possible to cite a respect in which the distribution of *bad* is not to that of *worse* as the distribution of *tall* is to that of *taller*, namely in the respect that in the one case there is and in the other case there is not an environment which, by insertion of the first form, yields the second form (which is a distributional feature of very many English positive-comparative pairs).

This observation prompts the further question: what, then, exactly is the statement of proportion intended to assert? Is the exception cited above the sole exception to an otherwise identical proportion? If we exclude by stipulation from the distribution that counts just any contexts which occur as morphs in the proportion, we presumably arrive at a statement of the following kind: 'Excluding the environment '. . .-*er*', the distribution of *bad* is to that of *worse* as that of *tall* is to that of *taller*, etc.' This is a statement which appears to make an empirical claim of a quite specific kind, yet when we come to consider how we might test it, it emerges that it is by no means clear precisely what the claim is.

According to (part of) Lyons's explanation, *worse* is alleged to differ distributionally from *taller* in the same way as *bad* differs from *tall*. But what, in turn, does that mean? Is to say that A differs distributionally from B in the same way as does C from D to say that any environment in which A occurs but not B is also an environment

---

[1] Lyons 1968, § 5.3.3.

[2] i.e. the invariant implied in saying that *a* is the comparative of *b* is identified by means of a distributional factor common to *a* and *b*: the *x* of which *a* and *b* are both forms is assumed to be characterized by this distributional property.

in which C occurs but not D? Or is it to say that those environments in which A occurs but not B are all and only the environments in which C occurs but not D? Or is it to say merely that a common feature can be found which characterizes those environments in which A occurs but not B and also those in which C occurs but not D? Or is it to say, even more merely, that a condition q can be established such that if q then either A but not B or C but not D? Lyons introduces the notion of 'similarity of distributional differences' by way of explanation: but until this notion itself is given some substantive content we cannot tell what it is that statements of distributional proportion assert.

However, it is not necessary to wait upon this enlightenment in order to see that, as a theory of M-relations, any attempted reduction to distributional factors has a fundamental flaw. In a proportion of the form 'A : x=C : D' where, for the sake of argument, the distributional relation of C to D is that of distributional identity, any candidate for x must be distributionally identical with A. If there is no form in the language with such a distribution, no x will be forthcoming. But if there is more than one such form, more than one x will be forthcoming. The same holds, *mutatis mutandis*, for cases of inclusive distribution, overlapping distribution and complementary distribution—in short, for whatever condition is imposed by the distributional proportion. It follows that the equation of M-relations with distributional relations yields absurd consequences, e.g. that any English form which happens to have a distribution identical with that of *bad* must (irrespective of form and meaning) have *worse* as its comparative. That there may be no such form in English does not affect the argument. The existence or non-existence of a form distributionally identical with *bad* is an empirical fact, and the theory provides no guarantee against contradiction by such facts. There is an assumption, in other words, that it is a property of natural languages that any two forms a and b uniquely paired by an M-relation are terms of a distributional relation which is matched in the case of at least one other pair of forms, and that either a or b is distributionally unique.[1] But this does not follow from any postulate of linguistic analysis; nor is any general reason apparent

---

[1] Except in the special case where the distributional proportion itself implies that a and b have identical distribution. But such a case will not, presumably, be taken as applicable where M-relations are concerned.

why it should be held to be true—except, circularly, to validate the theory of M-relations under discussion.

It might perhaps be urged that at least a semantically based theory of M-relations is no better off, since it leads to the parallel conclusion that any English form which happens to be synonymous with *bad* must have *worse* as its comparative. But no-one is obliged to argue that M-relations are determinable by semantic criteria alone: the point at issue is whether semantic criteria can be excluded. If anyone did maintain that an English adjective synonymous with *bad* must *ipso facto* have *worse* as its comparative, this would not be totally absurd, and well known facts of historical linguistics might be adduced to support it. A word *a* may 'take over' or 'assimilate' formally disparate elements from another word *b* if the semantic contrast between *a* and *b* lapses: e.g. the Spanish verb *ir* 'to go' (from Latin *ire*) has acquired present tense forms which originally belonged to Latin *vadere* (Sp. *voy*, *vas*, etc.), and this replacement presupposes a transitional state in which *eo* and *vado* were both 'first person present indicative' of *ire*.

Reverting now to the question of M-units, it is clear that if M-units may be set up to account for nonphonologically conditioned distributional patterns without recourse to meanings, then since such an enterprise needs no analysis of meanings, *a fortiori* it requires no concept of synonymy. This, however, leaves open the question of whether the enterprise *could* be carried out with M-units established on a semantic basis. It is not difficult to imagine a language structured in such a way that it would be quite impractical to attempt to state all or even most of the nonphonological sequence restrictions in terms of semantically determined units. (Such a language would have a 'third articulation', two of its three articulations being nonmeaningful.) A semantically based morphology (of which the general feasibility is not denied by 'distributionalists')[1] is intimately related to the assumption of dual articulation as a universal property of natural languages. But it does not follow from this assumption, granted its correctness, that units established on a semantic basis are

[1] Harris 1951, § 12.41 n. 67: '. . . there is in general a close correspondence between the morpheme division we might establish on a meaning basis and that which results from our distributional criteria. This is so because in general morphemes which differ in meaning will also differ in their environments, if we take sufficiently long environments and enough of them.' But this is not in fact a reason unless the point is tacitly conceded that natural languages have no important classes of nonmeaningful morphemes.

readily available for stating every grammatical fact. In support of this, one need look no further than the frequent discrepancies between proposed semantic definitions in morphology and some of the items occurring in natural languages to which the proposer is prepared (or not prepared) to apply the term. Such discrepancies usually arise from attempts either to 'stretch' the morpheme to cover units which it is morphologically useful to have included, but which happen not to be readily definable on a semantic basis, or else to 'shrink' it, so as to exclude troublesome items which appear, on semantic grounds, to have some claim to be included. Examples of 'morpheme-stretching' and 'morpheme-shrinkage' can be found in the presentations of semantically based morphology by Bloomfield, Bloch and Trager, and Hockett. Others could be cited, but the examples examined below are typical of the phenomenon. The relevant arguments clarify various points which have a bearing on questions of synonymy in relation to grammatical analysis.

The three definitions of the morpheme already cited—(i) 'a linguistic form which bears no partial phonetic-semantic resemblance to any other form', (ii) 'any form . . . which cannot be divided into smaller meaningful parts', and (iii) 'the smallest individually meaningful elements in the utterances of a language'—are by no means equivalent, but share a common appeal to semantic considerations. Definitions (ii) and (iii) require us to be able to decide simply whether or not certain items are meaningful, whereas (i) imposes the further requirement of determining a likeness of meaning between items (assuming that to speak of a semantic resemblance is not merely to speak of a resemblance which consists simply in being meaningful). However, the envisaged applications of (ii) and (iii) also involve this further requirement, as will become apparent below.

Definition (i)—Bloomfield's—assumes that we are dealing with meaningful expressions to which a determinate phonological form is assignable, and proposes a bipartition of this class of expressions into two disjoint classes (called 'simple' and 'complex'), using 'phonetic-semantic resemblance' as the criterion: '. . . some linguistic forms bear partial phonetic-semantic resemblances to other forms; examples are, *John ran, John fell, Bill ran, Bill fell*; *Johnny, Billy; playing, dancing; blackberry, cranberry; strawberry, strawflower.* A linguistic form which bears a partial phonetic-semantic resemblance to some other form is a *complex form.* The common part of any (two or more) complex forms is a linguistic form; it is a *constituent* (or *component*) of these complex forms.'[1] The constituents in the examples quoted are said to be: *John, ran, Bill, fell, play, dance, black, berry, straw, flower, cran-, -y,* and *-ing.*

The requirements of morphological analysis as envisaged in the foregoing statement appear to be three. 1. The linguist must be able to determine with respect to any given linguistic form whether that form is simple or complex. 2. In order to satisfy himself that it is complex he must be able, in the simplest type of case, to analyse it as a bipartite form *ab*, and to show that either *a* or *b* occurs elsewhere in the language as a linguistic form or part of a linguistic form. 3. In order to satisfy himself that it is simple, he must be able to show that the form does not yield to analysis in such a way that at least one part occurs elsewhere in the language as a linguistic form or part of a linguistic form. An assumption underlying these requirements is that a linguistic form is determinate with respect to meaning, and that this meaning is ascertainably constant for all instances of the linguistic form.

A somewhat different assumption is made in Bloch and Trager's presentation of definition (ii):

'As we examine the recorded utterances of an informant or a speech community, we note that the same or similar forms recur again and again with the same or similar meanings. Thus, the utterances of an English-speaking informant will contain many instances of such forms as *yes, person, I think so, out of town,* each time with about the same meanings, and also such different but phonemically related forms as *play, plays, played, playing,* or *ride, rides, rode, ridden, riding,* or *man, manly, mannish,* or *conceive, perceive, conception, perception, perceptive,* with different but related meanings.

'On the basis of such recurrence, we analyze the utterances into fractions of various lengths, each with a more or less constant meaning. Any fraction that can be spoken alone with meaning in normal speech is a FREE FORM; a fraction that never appears by itself with meaning is a BOUND FORM. All the examples in the preceding paragraph are free forms; *per-, con-, -ing, -ly, -ish, -ceive, -tion* are bound forms.'[2]

A feature of this account is its supposition that morphological

<hr>

[1] Bloomfield 1935, p. 161.
[2] Bloch and Trager 1942, § 4.2.

analysis has a certain semantic discovery structure. Some semantic information (about sameness or similarity or relatedness of meanings of expressions) is assumed to be available to empirical observation, and on the basis of this information the linguist constructs hypotheses about meanings not 'observable', namely those of the constituents of the expressions whose meanings are already known. The morpheme is the unit reached when factorial analysis of known or hypothesized items with their meanings can proceed no further.

A similar concept of the morpheme as the ultimate unit arrived at by a process of factorial analysis lies behind definition (iii)—Hockett's. The twin tests he suggests for the identification of any segment of a sentence as a morpheme are these: (I) that the segment recur in other utterances 'with approximately the same meaning', and (II) that it should not be the case that the recurring segment can 'be broken into smaller pieces, each of which recurs with approximately the same meaning, in such a way that the meaning of the whole form is related to the meanings of the smaller pieces.'[1] By these criteria, it is claimed, English *older* consists of two morphemes, one recurring in e.g. *oldster*, *oldest* and the other in e.g. *younger*, *finer*, while *sister* is monomorphemic, since neither *sist-er* nor any other division gives units which can plausibly be identified as having 'reasonable similarity of meaning' with phonemically comparable units in other utterances.

The definitions discussed above and their application to the morphological analysis of natural languages give rise to various important questions concerning identification of meanings. One which may profitably be discussed here concerns so-called 'unique' morphemes, since what is at issue in this case is the legitimacy of applying what purports to be a meaning-based definition of the morpheme in such a way as to yield criteria for identification of meanings, which will, in turn, enable certain otherwise excluded items to be classified as morphemes.

Unique morphemes make their appearance in morphological analysis as presented both by Bloomfield and by Hockett, and the justification given for their recognition is as follows.

1. (Bloomfield) '... having heard the form *cranberry*, we soon recognize the component *berry* in other forms, such as *blackberry*, and may even hear it spoken alone, but with the other component of *cranberry* we shall have no such luck. Not only do we wait in vain to

[1] Hockett 1958, § 14.1

hear an isolated *cran*, but, listen as we may, we never hear this element outside the one combination *cranberry*, and we cannot elicit from the speakers any other form which will contain this element *cran-*. As a practical matter, observing languages in the field, we soon learn that it is unwise to try to elicit such forms: our questions confuse the speakers, and they may get rid of us by some false admission, such as, "Oh, yes, I guess *cran* means red". If we avoid this pitfall, we shall come to the conclusion that the element *cran-* occurs only in the combination *cranberry*. However, since it has a constant phonetic form, and since its meaning is constant, in so far as a *cranberry* is a definite kind of *berry*, different from all other kinds, we say that *cran-*, too, is a linguistic form.'[1]

2. (Hockett) 'Occasionally, after we have extracted all the morphemes from some utterances by successive applications of Tests I and II [2] we seem to have something left over. Consider, for example,

[2] *Pléase páss the [3]cránbèrries[1]* ↓

The last word of this sentence can obviously be broken into *cranberry* and a morpheme /z/ meaning "plural". *Cranberry*, in turn, seems clearly to contain an element /bèrij/ which recurs in *strawberry, raspberry, gooseberry, blackberry, blueberry*, and so on. But how about *cran-*? We look in vain for any recurrence of *cran-* with anything like the meaning it has in *cranberry*.

A strict adherence to Tests I and II would therefore force us to take *cranberry* as a single morpheme. Yet this is obviously undesirable. In the first place, the identity of the second part of *cranberry* is hardly subject to doubt. In the second place, *cran-* clearly carries a meaning, even if the element occurs nowhere save in this one combination. Cranberries are different from strawberries, raspberries, gooseberries, and so on; the meaning of *cran-* is therefore whatever it is which differentiates cranberries from those other kinds of berries. It might be hard to describe this meaning, but it is easily demonstrated in a fruit market.

What we do under such circumstances is to recognize the element in question as a morpheme of a rather special kind—a *unique* morpheme. The recognition of such special morphemes does not

---

[1] Bloomfield 1935, p. 160.　[2] Cf. p. 66.

require any modification of our definition, but only calls for a slight change in the way we apply Tests I and II.'[1]

The question of unique morphemes is of interest because it points up a conflict between the enterprise of giving a semantically based definition of the morpheme and the desideratum that morphological analysis should be an analysis without residue. For if it proves possible to analyse an expression into *ab* such that *a* clearly occurs elsewhere with the same meaning, but *b* does not appear to, then we have the choice either of saying that there is a residue *b* whose status is unaccounted for, or else of declaring *b* a morpheme. What is dubious is whether we can opt for this latter alternative while maintaining unchanged or unsupplemented our original definition of the morpheme. It is the attempt to do this which leads Bloomfield and Hockett to deploy some very bad arguments.

Bloomfield contends that the meaning of *cran-* is constant 'in so far as a *cranberry* is a definite kind of *berry*', thus committing the double error of nonsense and *non sequitur*. What makes sense (and is true) is not that a *cranberry* is a kind of *berry*, but that a cranberry is a kind of berry. But it does not follow from that, nor from the fact that *cranberry* and *berry* are words for cranberries and berries respectively, that the meaning of *cran-* is constant. For it does not follow, *quod erat demonstrandum*, that *cran-* has a meaning at all (unless we define 'having a meaning' in such a way that being a unique element of the kind described is a sufficient condition for having a meaning—which would be clearly circular in the present instance).

Hockett, on the other hand, claims that since cranberries are different from strawberries, raspberries, gooseberries, etc., the meaning of *cran-* is therefore 'whatever it is which differentiates cranberries from these other kinds of berries'. Here, Bloomfield's *non sequitur* is compounded by a further *non sequitur*, namely the identification of the meaning of *cran-* with the whole set of differentiae of cranberries as a subclass of berries.[2] For there is no reason, granted that *cran-* has a meaning, why that meaning should be equated with

---

[1] Hockett 1958, § 14.2

[2] It is not entirely clear whether Hockett's thesis is that, or whether he holds the meaning of *cran-* to be whatever differentiates cranberries from other berries having names ending in *-berry*. He seems at times to be advancing the former and at times the latter view, without apparently realizing that this is to ascribe two different meanings to *cran-*.

all rather than any of the differentiae of the subclass of cranberries, nor, further, why we are obliged to equate it with a differentia of cranberries at all. (*Cran-* might be, as Bloomfield's hypothetical informant suggested, an otherwise unattested morpheme meaning e.g. 'red'.) The method of assigning meanings by simple 'semantic subtraction' is open to the objection levelled by Bazell[1] against Z. S. Harris's proposal that 'the meaning of *blue* in *blueberry* might be said to be the meaning of *blueberry* minus the meaning of *berry*': 'one could give any element whatever a meaning in this sense: e.g. the meaning of *b* in *beat* would be the difference between the meaning of *beat* and the meaning of *eat*.' Should it be replied that this reductio ad absurdum is unfair, since there is no presumption that the meanings of *beat* and *eat* are related, it would than be legitimate to point out that the *blueberry* example trades on the opposite presumption, namely that the meanings of *blueberry* and *berry* indeed are related. Applied without any such presumption, the method of 'semantic subtraction' yields trivial results: e.g. the meaning of *blue* in *blueberry* is the meaning of *blueberry* minus the meaning of *berry*, and, on the other hand, the meaning of *berry in blueberry* is the meaning of *blueberry* minus the meaning of *blue*.

Even if the semantic identity between *berry* standing alone and the second elements in *blueberry* and *cranberry* be conceded, the operation of 'semantic subtraction' is on no sounder theoretical footing. For, in general, for any bipartite meaningful expression *ab* where *a* but not *b* recurs with the same meaning elsewhere, it does not follow that *b* has a meaning. The fact that the language may have comparable expressions of the form *ac*, *ad*, etc., where both elements recur with the same meanings elsewhere, affords no demonstration of the meaningfulness of *b* in *ab*, since it does not follow from any postulate of linguistic analysis that related expressions must have identical semantic structures. In assigning a meaning to *b*, the linguist in fact yields to the same temptation as Bloomfield's informant —to be rid of the embarrassing question 'What does it mean?'.

There are other awkward cases which semantically based morphology seeks either to accommodate or to dismiss by disregarding its own proclaimed definition of the morpheme.

One such case is exemplified by series of forms such as: 1. *slime, slush, slop, slobber, slip, slide, slurp, slick*. 2. *flash, flare, flame, flicker, flimmer*.

[1] Bazell 1954, p. 330.

—where the members do seem to bear a phonetic-semantic resemblance to one another, which might be stated in the instances quoted as

[sl-]='smoothly wet'

and   [fl-]='moving light'.

Bloomfield recognizes such elements as 'root-forming morphemes'.[1] He does not, however, isolate similarly an initial element [n-]= 'negation' in such a series as: 3. *no, not, none, nor, never, neither*.[2] But in terms of the definition of the morpheme as a linguistic form which bears no partial phonetic-semantic resemblance to any other, series 1, 2 and 3 stand or fall together.

Nida, on the other hand, refuses to recognize the elements [sl-] and [fl-] of series 1 and 2 as morphemes, because in spite of the 'partial phonetic-semantic resemblances', the elements in question 'do not occur with free forms or with forms which occur in other combinations'.[3]

Two observations are in order concerning this objection. First, it is in fact not a valid objection to such cases as *none, nor, never, neither* (where *one, ever, either* presumably qualify as free forms) nor even to cases such as *flash* (in view of *bash, clash, crash, dash,* where [-aʃ]='violent movement'). Second, valid or not, the objection appeals to a principle which has no justification in terms of the given definition of the morpheme, i.e. the principle that elements not occurring in combination with free forms or with forms occurring in other combinations are not morphemes.

A further type of 'awkward case' is exemplified by such series as:

1. *conceive, deceive, perceive, receive.*
2. *attend, contend, distend, pretend.*
3. *adduce, conduce, deduce, induce, produce, reduce.*

—where the usual view taken by advocates of semantically based morphology is to regard elements such as *con-, de-, re-, -ceive, -tend, -duce* as morphemes, in spite of the difficulty of determining a semantic similarity. Bloomfield concedes that 'it seems impossible . . . to set up any consistent meaning' for such elements[4]; but does not tell us why in that case they should be regarded as morphemes. Nida reasons as follows: 'The prefix *con-* occurs only in combinations, e.g. *conceive, consume, contain, condense,* but the form *dense* occurs in isolation. This provides justification for considering *con-* a morpheme.

---

[1] Bloomfield 1935, p. 245.   [2] Bloomfield 1935, p. 244.
[3] Nida 1949, p. 61.   [4] Bloomfield 1935, p. 154.

Added evidence is available in the fact that the stem forms occur in other combinations, e.g. *perceive, resume, detain*.[1] All that is missing here is the explanation of why anyone should regard *con-* as a morpheme *for that reason*. For no attempt is made to find the semantic element of a presumed phonetic-semantic resemblance theoretically required for establishing morpheme status.

Unsatisfactory analyses of the kind discussed above might lead one to question whether a definition of the morpheme based on 'phonetic-semantic resemblance' can be viable, since its champions are evidently so hard put to it to give an account of awkward cases. It is possible, on the other hand, that the definition merits vindication at the expense of its champions. One might come to the conclusion that there is nothing wrong with the definition, but a great deal wrong with the way its proponents pay it lip service in theory but deny it in practice. Perhaps all that is needed to set matters right is a consistent application of the definition in various types of case.

Some of the arguments advanced by 'distributionalists' may be met in this way. For example, the case is cited of 'empty' morphs such as the *to* in English *I tried to swim*, which is simply present by requirement of English syntax, and thus held to be a counterexample to the thesis that morphemes are minimal meaningful units. The answer to this—if the charge of meaninglessness is conceded—is to withdraw the proposition that *to* is a morpheme.[2] For what is objectionable is not the intolerable consequences of denying so-called 'empty' morphs morphemic status, but the inconsistency involved in swelling the morpheme inventory of a language by the addition of admittedly meaningless members.

Quite a different objection, on the other hand, would be the objection that a definition of the morpheme in terms of 'phonetic-semantic resemblance' is incapable of consistent application. The chief ground on which this objection might be raised is that since neither 'phonetic resemblance' nor 'semantic resemblance' are defined in any very precise way, it seems impossible to decide, except *ad hoc* in different cases, what constitutes a phonetic-semantic

---

[1] Nida 1949, p. 59.

[2] Weinreich 1963, § 1.2 meets the objection in a different way by contending that 'empty' morphs are 'an artifact of an Item-and-Arrangement grammar: in an IP grammar, they are not "empty", but are the segmental markers of a transformation process'. It might still be objected that this is to fill the 'emptiness' with quite a different concept of 'meaning'.

resemblance. Those who try to maintain a semantic justification for the morpheme status of elements like *to* sometimes lay themselves open to this objection. Gleason, for example, concedes that 'it is impossible to find a specific factor in the situation which can be considered as the "meaning" of *to*. Nevertheless, *to* does have a function, since without it **I want go* means nothing.'[1] But, of course, in *that* sense the *w* of *want* also has a function, and moreover can be found with the same form and function in many other English sentences (*I want treacle, I wish you'd stay* etc.).

As regards the element of phonetic resemblance in a 'phonetic-semantic resemblance', the objection raises a point of some significance in connexion with synonymy. It would presumably be possible for the Bloomfieldian to meet the objection by falling back, if pressed, on the notion of phonetic resemblance which no-one could reasonably question, i.e. phonemic identity. Now a grammar constructed on the basis of this interpretation of 'phonetic-semantic resemblance' would have no room for synonymity statements, i.e. there would be no cases in which the determination of M-units depended on deciding whether two phonologically different items were alike in meaning. But a further and related property of such a grammar would be that the difference between e.g. the noun forms *knife* and *knive* (as in *knives*) would be exactly on a par with the difference between, say *dock* and *dog*, these four forms counting as four different M-units.

In other words, without appeal to the notion of synonymy in a grammar based on 'phonetic-semantic resemblance', the distinction between morph and morpheme collapses. Synonymity statements are required in Bloomfieldian grammar precisely to support the contention that a given morpheme may appear in various forms[2], a requirement which makes Bloomfield's theoretical rejection of synonymity[3] all the more paradoxical.

The concept of synonymy plays a somewhat different role in semantically based morphology if the morpheme is defined not in terms of 'phonetic-semantic resemblance', but as a unit determined conjointly by semantic and distributional criteria, as e.g. in the account of morphological analysis given by Gleason.[4] Here the function of the concept is precisely to allow morphological analysis to proceed without any reliance at all on phonetic or phonological

---

[1] Gleason 1966, § 5. 11.   [2] Bloomfield 1935, p. 164.
[3] Cf. pp. 6–7.   [4] Gleason 1966.

resemblance between morphs. The point is perhaps best illustrated by reference to one of Gleason's definitions. Two (or more) morphs are said to represent the same morpheme if they have 'some common range of meaning', and if they are 'in complementary distribution conditioned by some phonologic feature'.[1] (Such a case would be the English noun plurals /-z/, /-s/ and /-iz/.) It is clear that the enterprise of constructing a grammar here depends on being able to identify various morphs (e.g. /-z/, /-s/, /-iz/) as having the same meaning (say, 'more than one'); but provided we can do this we need not bother about any lack of phonological resemblance between the morphs in question. Thus although the case is different from that of setting up M-units on the basis of 'phonetic-semantic resemblance', it is again the appeal to synonymy which supports the distinction between morph (or allomorph) and morpheme.

It may perhaps be questioned whether a proviso as strong as that of synonymity of the morphs in question is required in the cases under discussion. Would it not be sufficient to allow that e.g. /-z/, /-s/ and /-iz/, or *duke* and *duch-*, may differ in meaning, provided any such differences are granted to play no part in determining the selection of these morphs as elements in English sentences? We might conceive of these cases as ones in which, to adopt Hockett's words, the choice 'is made *for* the speaker rather than *by* him',[2] or— we must add—if *by* him, then not as a *semantic* choice. This would allow the distinction between morph and morpheme to be drawn, and drawn on a semantic basis, but without invoking synonymy.

Along these lines, the concept of morpheme alternance might be explicated for purposes of semantically based morphology as the concept of the relation between members of a class of phonologically differing forms which share a common meaning, and between which the language affords the speaker no grammatically indeterminate semantic choice. (That is to say, either there is no choice (because by grammatical rule all members of the class but one are excluded), or, if more than one member of the class is grammatically permissible, then it makes no semantic difference which of those permitted is chosen.)

This appears to cover all the usual examples adduced in discussions of morphological analysis. And yet there is something very curious about this concept. It may be observed, first of all, that if we

[1] Gleason 1966, § 7.3.   [2] Hockett 1958, § 15.1.

strengthen the first semantic requirement so that instead of speaking forms which 'share a common meaning' we speak of forms 'which are identical in meaning', then the second requirement becomes redundant, since if the forms have the same meaning, then *ipso facto* a speaker has no semantic choice. (We thus reintroduce the proviso of synonymity.)

On the other hand, it is difficult to see how the concept of alternance as stated could be of any practical use in morphological analysis unless supplemented by criteria for determining sameness of meanings. Attention is rarely paid to such criteria, and when it is the results are palpably inadequate. For example, the demonstration given by Hockett[1] that the English noun plurals /-s/ and /-z/ have no discoverable difference in meaning is question-begging. What Hockett successfully demonstrates is simply that they occur in complementary distribution. But it is hardly surprising that a substitution test of the kind Hockett uses should *fail* to discover a difference in meaning between forms in complementary distribution: on the contrary, it must fail. To take such a test seriously involves supposing that complementarity of distribution is a sufficient condition of synonymity. But anyone who supposed *that* could easily demonstrate that e.g. English *the* and *'s* are synonymous. Moreover, if such a test is to be treated as decisive, it would be simpler to stop talking about differences of meaning and merely rely on the test. For the test is applicable, irrespective of what we suppose it to be a test of.

But normally no-one goes even to the trouble taken by Hockett to exhibit the supposed synonymy of allomorphs of the same morpheme: at best we are offered a brief identification of 'the meaning' they are said to share (e.g. 'more than one' for noun plurals) and for the rest it is simply assumed that any differences of meaning are morphologically irrelevant.

If we relied simply on the discovery of a 'common meaning', however, we should be forced to conclude that e.g. *knives* and *forks* contained not one but two pairs of morphs with common meanings. For a common meaning can be stated for each pair (e.g. 'implement', 'more than one') and the grammatical rules of English never offer a choice between the morphs in question (*knive*: *fork* and /-z/ : /-s/). It is no objection to this example to point out that everyone knows

[1] Hockett 1958, § 15.1.

that the plural of *knife* differs in meaning from the plural of *fork*. Doubtless they do differ, and this is the point of the example. What is illustrated thereby is that there is no way of saying just how much the two morphs must have semantically in common, short of the synonymity proviso.

But that is the beginning—not the end—of the underlying task inseparable from the whole of semantically based morphology, namely to define the dimension(s) of communicational relevance to be subsumed under 'meaning'.

If the objective of syntactic description is taken to be simply the specification of all and only the grammatical concatenations of morphs in the language, the question whether two such concatenations are synonymous, like all other questions about the semantic properties of grammatical sequences, falls outside the province of syntactic analysis. Questions of meaning become relevant, however, if we take it to be part of the function of a syntax to assign structural descriptions to the specified grammatical sequences. For it may be asked of any given sequence whether it has one or more than one grammatical analysis, and the fact that a sentence is or is not ambiguous is here of some importance. E.g. the fact that the German sentence *Das ist natürlich genug* is assigned two structural descriptions is directly related to the fact that it is ambiguous.[1] Transformational grammarians, following Chomsky, have normally included non-lexical ambiguities as being among the facts to be accounted for by an

---

[1] Bach 1964, § 3.3 gives the analyses:

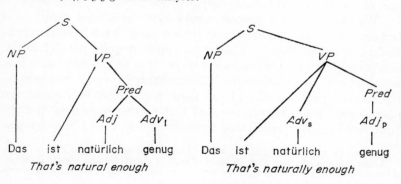

F

adequate grammar,[1] and in accounting for these have implicitly provided explanations for certain synonymities and nonsynonymities as well.[2]

The relation between synonymy and grammatical ambiguity may conveniently be discussed by taking as a starting point the following proposition:

A1 'If *axy* and *bxy* are synonymous, then either both are grammatically ambiguous, or neither.'

That is to say, if the sequences $a+x+y$ and $b+x+y$ are both syntactic arrangements permitted by the grammar of the language, and we have a guarantee that the resultant expressions *axy* and *bxy* do not differ in meaning, then it cannot be the case that only one of these expressions is grammatically ambiguous.

A1 appears to correspond to the basic position adopted by transformational grammarians, as witnessed by such statements as the following:

'Occasionally, a grammar may permit us to construct nonequivalent derivations for a given sentence. Under these circumstances, we say that we have a case of "constructional homonymity", and if our grammar is correct, this sentence of the language should be ambiguous.'[3] 'Obviously, not all kinds of ambiguity will be analyzable in syntactic terms. For example, we would not expect a grammar to explain the referential ambiguity of "son"—"sun", "light" (in color, weight), etc.'[4]

'We can test the adequacy of a given grammar by asking whether or not each case of constructional homonymity is a real case of ambiguity and each case of the proper kind of ambiguity is actually a case of constructional homonymity.'[5]

'We can state as a general requirement for a total theory of a language that any ambiguous sequence must have several representations in the theory. This requirement is quite parallel to the condition placed on a phonological theory that no two sequences that are 'different' (i.e. consistently distinguishable by a pair test) may be represented phonemically in the same way. That is, beyond the phonological level, we can demand that no two sequences that are "different" may be represented in the same way, even if they happen

---

[1] Chomsky 1957, §§ 4.1 and 8.1. Bach 1964, §§ 1.2 and 5.2.
[2] For example, the fact that, in spite of certain structural and lexical parallels, *old men's shoes* and *men's old shoes* do not receive identical semantic interpretations is very well accounted for by the grammatical ambiguity of the former.
[3] Chomsky 1957, § 4.1.   [4] Chomsky 1957, § 8.1 n. 1.   [5] Chomsky 1957, § 8.1.

to have the same phonemic shape. Some of these differences will be accounted for by a theory of language usage. . . . Some, presumably, will be accounted for by a semantic theory: *Look at the table* is ambiguous only because *table* has several meanings, e.g., 'mathematical table', 'dinner table'. In the realm of grammar proper, different representations may exist . . . on the level of phrase structure (different P markers for the same string). They may also exist in the transformational level, as in . . . *I don't approve of his cooking*, or *John is crazy to go.*'[1]

In discussing A1, it may be taken for granted that if, in the context '. . . *xy*', *a* is lexically ambiguous but *b* is not, then *axy* and *bxy* will not be synonymous; but then the grammar is not expected to account for the ambiguity.

The case for believing A1 to be correct—if it is correct—depends on the semantic implications of the term 'grammatical ambiguity', which must now be examined.

Some clarification of the distinction between grammatical and lexical ambiguity is first necessary. It may be and often is the case that a grammatical ambiguity involves the assignment of two meanings to a single lexical item. For example, in *I saw logs*[2] the lexical item *saw* may be assigned two distinct meanings, but also two distinct grammatical classifications ('past tense' of *see* vs. 'present tense' of *saw*). Thus although the ambiguity centres about one particular lexical item, the grammatical analysis of the sentence containing it is affected. This is the justification for calling *I saw logs* a 'syntactical ambiguity'[3]; the sentence yields the two phrase markers

$$(1) \quad ((I)_{NP}((PAST)_{Aux}(see)_V(logs)_{NP})_{VP})_S$$

and $(2) \quad ((I)_{NP}((saw)_V(logs)_{NP})_{VP})_S$

If we prefer to reserve the term 'syntactical ambiguity' for bracketing ambiguities (constructional homonymities), an alternative would be to call *I saw logs* a 'distributional ambiguity' since, as Lyons observes,[4] the ambiguity in such cases is a function of the distributional classification of the item involved. (Here *saw* belongs to two distributional classes, in one of which it has such co-members as *heard, found, brought*, and in the other such co-members as *hear, find, bring*.)

When 'lexical ambiguity' is contrasted with 'grammatical ambiguity' the implication usually is that no grammatical factors are

[1] Bach 1964, § 5.2.
[2] An example discussed by Katz and Martin 1967, p. 484.
[3] As do Katz and Martin, loc. cit.   [4] Lyons 1968, § 6.1.3.

appealed to in explaining the ambiguity of the expression in which the lexically ambiguous item occurs. The connexion between lexical and grammatical (syntactical) ambiguity is analysed along these lines by Katz and Postal as follows:

'A lexical item is ambiguous when it has more than one sense. Ambiguity at the lexical level is the source of semantic ambiguity at the sentence level. Thus, a necessary but not sufficient condition for a syntactically unambiguous sentence to be semantically ambiguous is that it contain at least one ambiguous lexical item. For example, the source of the semantic ambiguity in the sentence

(2) he enjoys wearing a light suit in the summer

is the ambiguity of the lexical item *light*. Since an adequate dictionary entry for a lexical item must mark every one of its senses, the dictionary entry for *light* must represent it as at least two-ways ambiguous, in terms of two readings which differ from each other in that one contains the semantic marker (Color) but not the semantic marker (Weight) and the other contains (Weight) but not (Color). Since there is nothing in (2) to exclude either one of these readings as genuine readings for the occurrence of *light*, the sentence is semantically ambiguous, one term of this ambiguity stemming from each of these readings.

However, the presence of an ambiguous lexical item in a syntactically unambiguous sentence is not a sufficient condition for that sentence to be semantically ambiguous. For example, although the sentence

(3) the stuff is light enough to carry[1]

contains an occurrence of the ambiguous lexical item *light*, it is not itself ambiguous because *light enough to carry* is not understood to mean 'light enough in color to be carried'. Thus when there is an ambiguous lexical item in a semantically unambiguous sentence, either the syntactic properties of the sentence or the meanings of the other constituents prevent the ambiguous lexical item from contributing more than one of its senses to the meaning of the whole sentence.'[2]

The example of *light* illustrates the residual character of the

---

[1] Katz and Postal's example here is poorly chosen, since it appears that '. . . *enough to carry*' must be grammatically ambiguous: i.e. somewhere in the history of the sentence there has occurred conflation which has obscured the modal difference between 'it is possible to carry *x*' and 'it is desirable (advantageous, opportune etc.) to carry *x*'. Hence the sentence, contrary to Katz and Postal's interpretation, can have the reading 'the stuff is light enough (in colour) to carry'.

[2] Katz and Postal 1964, p. 15.

notion of lexical ambiguity, being dependent on the assumption that the derivations for sentences containing *light* are identical in respect of the way in which they eventually produce the formative *light*. But a detailed analysis of English might perhaps uncover grounds for assigning two syntactic markers to the lexicon entry for *light* (? 'Appearance Adj.' vs. 'Substance Adj.'), and then the need to consider *light* a case of lexical ambiguity would lapse.

An analysis which appears to allow the possibility of contradicting A1 is offered by Lyons in his version of the distinction between grammatical and semantic ambiguity:

> 'Let us assume, for the sake of the argument, that neither *fresh fruit market* nor *new fruit market* has more than one interpretation: from the semantic point of view, we will say that they are not ambiguous. Are they grammatically ambiguous? Is the constituent-structure *fresh (fruit market)*, in the one case, and *(new fruit) market*, in the other, grammatically acceptable? To answer these questions we must of course refer to some explicit grammar of English. It is clear that, in general, the bracketing $A+(N_1+N_2)$ is acceptable if the first noun can combine with the second *(fruit market)* and if the adjective can combine with the second noun *(new market, ? fresh market)*; and the bracketing $(A+N_1)+N_2$ is acceptable if the first noun can combine with the second noun and if the adjective can combine with the first noun *(fresh fruit, ? new fruit)*. . . . Any phrase of the form $A+N_1+N_2$ will be given two grammatical analyses, unless the grammar and the lexicon to which we refer prohibits explicitly the combination of the adjective in question with one or other of the nouns.'[1]

Let us now develop Lyons's example in the following way: first, by assuming fulfilment of the condition mentioned in Lyons's last sentence, namely that the grammar and lexicon explicitly prohibit the combination of one adjective with one (but not the other) of the nouns in question, and second, by stipulating not merely that *fresh fruit market* and *new fruit market* are semantically unambiguous but also that they are synonymous.

It would now follow from Lyons's argument that, unless there is a contradiction in the stipulations, we have a case where *axy* and *bxy* are synonymous but only one is grammatically ambiguous.

That there is no contradiction in the stipulations may be con-

[1] Lyons 1968, § 6.1.3.

cluded from the following considerations. 1. If we were committed to supposing that the synonymy of *fresh fruit market* and *new fruit market* was the result of the independent synonymy of *fresh* and *new*, then it might be queried why one of these adjectives could qualify one but not the other of the nouns. But there seems to be no general reason to deny that synonymous complex expressions may be made up of lexical items which, considered in isolation, or in other combinations, are not synonymous. The unambiguous and identical semantic interpretation of two phrases or sentences is not a sufficient condition for identity of the lexical entries of their corresponding lexical items. 2. There seems to be no general reason to deny that a lexical item which is grammatically permissible in a given context C_1 may not be so in a partially similar context C_2. 3. The stipulations made involve no stronger claims than those covered by the preceding two points, namely that (i) *axy* and *bxy* may be synonymous even if *a* and *b* are not, and (ii) *axy* and *bxy* may be grammatical when *ax*, or *ay*, or *bx*, or *by* are not.

It now appears that by following Lyons's argument we have reached a conclusion which conflicts with A1, and indeed this is so if the term 'grammatically ambiguous' in A1 is to be given the sense which Lyons implicitly gives it in answering the question 'Are they grammatically ambiguous?'.

But there are reasons for rejecting the way Lyons interprets this question, and hence also for rejecting the answer he gives. The main objection may be stated concisely as follows. Lyons assumes the question to mean 'Are they ambiguous according to a grammar?' and gives the trivial and unhelpful answer 'They are if the grammar says so'. Whereas if the question is to have any linguistic interest at all, it must mean 'What linguistic facts would lead one to construct a grammar which represented them as ambiguous?'. Lyons's answer —if it is read as an answer to *that* question—is perhaps less trivial, but now becomes baffling. For we are being told that the ungrammaticality of *new fruit* (in isolation) should preclude the assignment of grammatical ambiguity to *new fruit market*—without, however, being told why. But that is precisely what we want to know in order to clarify the notion of grammatical ambiguity.[1]

---

[1] Putting forward a solution for a particular example, in advance of any general principle, simply constitutes a retreat into obscurity, i.e. what is now unclear is what constitutes the incompatibility between the ungrammaticality of *new fruit* and the grammatical—as opposed to semantic—ambiguity of *new fruit market*. For it will hardly do to say that 'grammatical ambiguity of *axy*' just *is* 'independent combinability of *a*, *x* and *y*'.

An alternative interpretation of 'grammatical ambiguity' is available, but it leans too heavily on semantic considerations to be acceptable to one who adopts Lyons's position. According to this alternative interpretation grammatical ambiguity is a property of certain types of construction, and any individual construction either belongs to a grammatically ambiguous type (in which case it counts individually as grammatically ambiguous) or it does not. On this view, the ungrammaticality of *new fruit* would not count against the grammatical ambiguity of *new fruit market*: for the question to be answered is not 'Is *new fruit* grammatical?' but 'Does *new fruit market* belong to a grammatically ambiguous construction-type?', where 'grammatically ambiguous construction-type' is defined as one in which semantically unambiguous elements may be combined into semantically ambiguous complexes.

To indicate the general reasons for adopting this definition (which places 'grammatical ambiguity' in a position of dependence on the prior notion of 'semantic ambiguity') it will be relevant to consider some grammatical ambiguities other than 'bracketing ambiguities'. Lyons distinguishes two further basic types of grammatical ambiguity, exemplified by *They can fish* and *amor Dei*, the former being a case of what was above termed 'distributional ambiguity' (*can* is both a modal auxiliary and a transitive verb, and *fish* both an intransitive verb and a noun), and the latter a case of 'transformational ambiguity' (*Deus amat.* vs. *Deum amat*).[1]

It is relevant to the problem under discussion to note that in drawing a distinction between such cases as types of grammatical ambiguity, there is already a certain amount of illicit trading on the notion of 'ambiguity'—illicit, that is to say, if we wish to maintain that semantic ambiguity and grammatical ambiguity are independent notions.

For example, although it may be convenient to speak of 'grammatical ambiguity' in cases when a position which can be occupied either by an A-class form or by a B-class form is in fact occupied by a form which belongs to both classes, it must be realized that strictly from the point of view of distribution of forms it is nonsense to apply the term 'ambiguity'. For there is no sense in which a form must be *either* A-class *or* B-class (exclusive disjunction) to occur in such a position: we could equally well set up an AB-class limited to forms which occur both in A-class positions and in B-class positions, and

---

[1] Lyons 1968, § 6.1.3, § 6.6.2.

the question whether a form occurring in a position open to both is an A-class form or a B-class form would then simply not arise. The term 'ambiguity' in such cases tacitly appeals to the fact that in sentences where an AB-class form occupies an A-class position it will often receive a different semantic interpretation from that which it receives when occupying a B-class position; with the result that when it occupies an AB-class position one asks which semantic interpretation it should have. No-one, presumably, would speak of 'ambiguity' either (i) if a position is filled by a form which elsewhere occurs only in A-class (or only in B-class) positions, or (ii) if forms which may occur both in A-class positions and B-class positions receive exactly the same semantic interpretation in both types of position.

Or, to take a different type of case, if *men and old women* did not differ in meaning from *old men and old women* or from *old men and women* (i.e. if the adjective semantically applicable to both nouns could be syntactically preposed to either or to both) and if constructions of this type did not admit the interpretation whereby the adjective was semantically relevant to one noun only, then presumably no-one would regard *old men and women* as grammatically ambiguous. Yet it would remain true that *old men and women* could be treated as syntactically derived in more than one way (e.g. by deletion of the second *old* from *old men and old women*, or by preposition to *men and women*, or by fronting from *men and old women*). But if there is to be any point in speaking of 'ambiguity' there has to be some sense in which one construction subsumes the other two, and they are not just equal partners.

In general, it would seem that to maintain a distinction between grammatical and semantic ambiguity is legitimate only to the extent that knowledge of grammatical ambiguities may be explicated as nonsemantic (i.e. formal) linguistic knowledge. The question how far this 'extent' goes requires some consideration.

Knowledge of the grammaticality or otherwise of a sentence or construction must be counted formal knowledge, since it is knowledge of the combination rules governing sets of formally defined items (i.e. the words or morphs of the language). The knowledge which enables a speaker to segment utterances into constituent grammatical units is also to be counted formal knowledge, since it can be treated as knowledge of substitution procedures not presupposing any knowledge of the meanings of the items involved. In short, all knowledge of the nouns, adjectives, verbs, etc. of a language and their rules of combination may be regarded as knowledge of what may be substituted for what and in what contexts. But whether this includes knowledge of grammatical ambiguities is not immediately obvious.

It might appear that in some instances at least a case can be made for analysing knowledge of grammatical ambiguity as knowledge of relations between substitution constraints. E.g. knowledge of the grammatical ambiguity of *They can fish* might perhaps be said to be knowledge that in this sentence *can* and *fish* may each be replaced *salva grammaticalitate* by members of two different sets of expressions related in a certain way. If we call these sets of expressions '*can*-A', '*can*-B', '*fish*-A' and '*fish*-B', the rule is that '*can*-A' substitutes must go with '*fish*-A' substitutes and '*can*-B' substitutes with '*fish*-B' substitutes.[1] Knowledge of the grammatical ambiguity, it might be suggested, is simply knowledge of this rule, i.e. of a specific interdependence between the substitution possibilities for *can* and *fish*.

But grammatical ambiguity cannot simply be equated with interdependence between substitution patterns of morphs or words in a given sentence. For on the one hand there would seem to be cases of grammatically ambiguous sentences where no relevant interdependence obtains, while on the other hand there are cases of interdependence which do not correspond to grammatical ambiguity. An example of the former would be *I saw logs*, and of the latter *John bought it*. In the former instance, the grammatical ambiguity of *saw* (present tense of *saw* vs. past tense of *see*) matches no interdependence between the permissible substitutions for *saw* and the permissible substitutions for *I*, *log* or *-s*. In the case of *John bought it*, the following interdependence holds between substitutions for *bought* and substitutions for *it*: '*bought*-A' includes *ate*; '*bought*-B' includes *drank*; '*it*-A' includes *bread*; '*it*-B' includes *wine*. This rule expresses the fact that we cannot have **John drank bread*, nor **John ate wine*. Thus there is here a substitutional interdependence, but it does not seem to correspond to a grammatical ambiguity in *John bought it*.

More generally, a major difficulty in the way of explicating grammatical ambiguity in terms of membership of substitution sets is that each word in the language may be regarded as belonging to many overlapping substitution sets. The approach thus leads ultimately to the proposition that if a word belongs to *n* different substitution

---

[1] '*Can*-A' will include *may, could, will, . . .*; '*can*-B' will include *pack, sell, take, . . .* ; '*fish*-A' will include *go, come, stay, . . .*; '*fish*-B' will include *peas, beans, tomatoes, . . .*

sets in different contexts, and there is a context in which it may be replaced by any member of any of its n substitution sets, then in that context the word is n-ways grammatically ambiguous. Similarly, a word would be n-minus-x-ways grammatically ambiguous in contexts where it may be replaced by any member of n-minus-x of its substitution sets, and unambiguous where n-minus-x equals one. But since almost every sentence in every natural language would then turn out to be multiply grammatically ambiguous, this is presumably an account of 'grammatical ambiguity' which no-one would readily accept.

An alternative approach to the explication of grammatical ambiguity is by reference to an explicit set of generative rules for producing the sentences of the language. Then a sentence or constituent is unambiguous if the rules give only one way of generating it, and n-ways grammatically ambiguous if the rules give n ways of generating it. However, this account of grammatical ambiguity depends on there being guarantees that the rules do not contain either 'superfluous' ways of generating particular sentences, or 'insufficient' ways of generating particular sentences. But since the tests of 'superfluity' and 'insufficiency' are semantic tests,[1] this approach does not enable us to account for grammatical ambiguity without appeal to meanings.

The plausibility of a semantically based interpretation of grammatical ambiguity gains support from the difficulty of finding convincing counterexamples, i.e. intuitively clear cases of grammatical ambiguity where no systematic semantic ambiguity is generated. Examples which come to mind in this connexion—e.g. that of recursive co-ordinate constructions—seem to be cases in which any alleged 'grammatical ambiguity' is a product of the convention adopted for representing the grammar, and corresponds to no genuine item of linguistic knowledge at all.[2]

---

[1] The 'insufficiency' of rules which give only one way of generating *old men's shoes* is demonstrated by the fact that *old men's shoes* has two distinct semantic interpretations, given only one meaning each for *old*, *men's* and *shoes*. The 'superfluity' of rules which give fourteen different ways of generating *old men's shoes* is demonstrated by the fact that *old men's shoes* does not have fourteen distinct semantic interpretations.

[2] A grammar's ambiguous representation of *old men's shoes* corresponds to a genuine item of linguistic knowledge in that the competent speaker-hearer knows that *old* may go either with *men* or with *shoes*, whereas it would be nonsense to say that a grammar's ambiguous representation of *Tom and Dick and Harry* corresponds to the competent speaker-hearer's knowledge that *Dick* may go either with *Tom* or with *Harry*.

The above considerations weigh in favour of explicating grammatical ambiguity in terms of capacity to generate semantic ambiguities. Accordingly, the question whether *fresh fruit market* and *new fruit market* are grammatically ambiguous even if semantically unambiguous becomes the question whether the combination A+N+N is one able to combine semantically unambiguous items into semantically ambiguous complexes. This question will receive an affirmative answer if suitably ambiguous expressions of the type A+N+N can be found, where the ambiguity corresponds to the possibility of bracketing (A+N) +N or A+ (N+N), the same meanings being assigned to individual words in either case.[1]

Interpreting A1 in this sense, A1 states that if *axy* and *bxy* are synonymous, then it cannot be the case that only one of them belongs to a construction-type able to combine semantically unambiguous items into semantically ambiguous complexes. Now for this to be so, we have to take the assurance of synonymity to preclude the possibility that one expression but not the other instantiates a grammatical ambiguity which *in this instance* happens to be semantically inconsequential. An assurance merely of the 'synthetic synonymity' of *axy* and *bxy* (i.e. an assurance that the two expressions command the same semantic interpretation as wholes, irrespective of their internal structure) is insufficient to validate A1 in the light of the interpretation given above of 'grammatical ambiguity'. For it might be the case that *a* but not *b* belongs to a class of words which combine grammatically with members of the class to which *x* belongs, but that *in this instance* '*a+x*' has a meaning which, combined with the meaning of *y*, yields the same meaning 'M' for the whole expression *axy* as is independently yielded by combining the meaning of *a* with that of '*x+y*'. In such a case, the possibility of interpreting *axy* grammatically either as (*ax*)*y* or as *a*(*xy*) is semantically of no consequence, since *axy* means 'M' in either case.

The guarantee of 'synthetic synonymity' between *axy* and *bxy*, (here the guarantee that *axy* and *bxy* have only the meaning 'M') thus does not ensure parity of grammatical ambiguity between them. Can we, then, formulate a stronger condition which will validate A1?

We may usefully explore this question by drawing on the theoretical apparatus of generative grammar. Of particular relevance is the distinction of Katz and Postal between *sentence* and *sentoid* (the latter defined as a string of formatives with a unique associated

---

[1] Such expressions exist in English, e.g. *red wine punch, foreign book shop*.

structural description).[1] Taking *axy* and *bxy* as sentences, the possibility we are attempting to guard against is the possibility that *axy* (but not *bxy*) represents two sentoids, each of which receives the same derived reading as that for the sentoid corresponding to *bxy*. This possibility would be instantiated by a case[2] in which *axy* had only the P-markers

PM1 $(((a)_T(x)_U)_P(y)_Q)_{S1}$
and PM2 $((a)_R((x)_U(y)_Q)_P)_{S2}$
and *bxy* only the P-marker
PM3 $((b)_R((x)_U(y)_Q)_P)_{S3}$

and where S1, S2 and S3 were full paraphrases (fully synonymous) under Katz and Postal's definition

> D5 C and C' are *fully synonymous with respect to PM and PM'* if and only if the set of readings associated with the node labeled 'C' in PM and the set of readings associated with the node labeled 'C'' in PM' are identical; PM may equal PM'.[3]

But there is another possibility which would be equally damaging to A1. This is the possibility that *axy* (but not *bxy*) represents two sentoids, one of which happens to be semantically anomalous under Katz and Postal's definition

> D1 C is *semantically anomalous with respect to PM* if and only if the set of readings associated with the node labeled 'C' in PM contains no readings, i.e. is null.[4]

and the other of which receives a derived reading identical with that of the sentoid corresponding to *bxy*. This would be the case, in terms of the example just given, if in PM1 the node Q had a reading which failed to combine with the derived reading for P, and S2 and S3 were fully synonymous under D5.

The assurance of what was referred to above as the 'synthetic

---

[1] Katz and Postal 1964, pp. 23–27.
[2] The relevant P-markers may be diagrammed as follows:

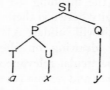 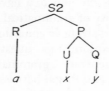 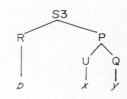

[3] Katz and Postal 1964, p. 27.   [4] Katz and Postal 1964, p. 26.

synonymity' of *axy* and *bxy* may be reformulated in Katz and Postal's terminology as an assurance that all pairs of nonanomalous sentoids for *axy* and *bxy* respectively are fully synonymous (are 'full paraphrases') and there is at least one such pair. But this condition is not strong enough to validate A1 because of the possibility of counterexamples of the kind just discussed.

The stronger condition which must be met to eliminate such counterexamples is clearly that *axy* and *bxy* should have the same number of sentoids and that it should be possible to put their respective sentoids in one-one correspondence, each such pair being fully synonymous under D5. Sentences (and, by extension, constituents of sentences) which meet this condition might be termed 'structurally synonymous'.

If an assurance of the synonymity of *axy* and *bxy* is taken to be an assurance of their 'structural synonymity' as defined above, then A1 is correct.

We are thus led to draw a distinction which it would have been irrelevant to introduce into a discussion of the role of synonymity statements at the phonological level, but which assumes importance in connexion with grammatical analysis.

It is not the only distinction of which this is true. Another is that between synonymous sentences which have different underlying P-markers and those which have the same underlying P-marker(s).

(1a) *He brought home some furze*
(1b) *He brought home some gorse*
(2a) *He wrapped the parcel up*
(2b) *He wrapped up the parcel*

If we assume the above pairs are synonymous pairs, then (1a) and (1b) are 'structurally synonymous' in the sense discussed i.e. they represent two fully synonymous sentoids. (2a) and (2b), on the other hand, presumably come not from underlying P-markers which happen to coincide in their semantic interpretation but from one and the same P-marker. Such pairs may be said to be 'intrinsically synonymous'.

Pairs like (2a) and (2b) are related by optional singulary transformations as defined by Katz and Postal:

'In earlier treatments of transformational grammar, such as Chomsky's in *Syntactic Structures*, optional singulary transformations had at least two distinct functions. First, they derived various distinct sentence types, questions, imperatives, negatives, etc., from

88   SYNONYMY AND LINGUISTIC ANALYSIS

one underlying declarative type. They thus had a substantive role in explaining differences in cognitive meaning between sentences of the same syntactic type. Second, singulary transformations related optional variants that were full paraphrases. These were intuitively stylistic variants of each other like

(133) a. all the men are married
b. the men are all married
c. he found out the truth
d. he found the truth out

In our discussion of the syntax of questions, imperatives, etc., we have given a great deal of support for a conception in which only the second function of singulary transformations survives. It therefore seems reasonable to say in general that the different outputs produced by optional singulary transformations are merely stylistic variants necessarily having the same cognitive meaning. Thus there can be a uniform characterization of the function of optional rules for both the syntactic and phonological components; such rules derive what is referred to in linguistics as *free variation*, and nothing else.'[1]

It may be noted that intrinsic synonymity of expressions is not the guarantee required to validate A1, but rather one condition which would validate

A2 If *abcd* and *abdc* are synonymous, then either both are grammatically ambiguous, or neither.

We do not, however, need a guarantee of intrinsic synonymity to rule out e.g. the possibility that *abdc* might, unlike *abcd*, be open to the bracketing *a(bd)c*. For that purpose structural synonymity of *abcd* and *abdc* would meet the requirement. Thus intrinsic synonymity of the two expressions is a sufficient but not a necessary condition for validation of A2.

The much discussed[2] synonymy of actives and their corresponding passives may be subsumed under 'intrinsic synonymy', although a case can be made out for treating e.g.

(3a) *John kissed Mary*
and   (3b) *Mary was kissed by John*

---

[1] Katz and Postal 1964, pp. 112–113. In connexion with 'free variation', however, it should be noted that whereas in syntax the truth of the statement that *a* and *b* are synonymous is a necessary condition of the *correctness* of treating *a* and *b* as 'free variants' (in the sense of being 'merely stylistic variants' of the same sentence), the same statement assumes, at the phonological level, the *incorrectness* of treating the phonetic realizations of *a* and *b* as free variants.
[2] Chomsky 1957, § 9.2.7, Katz and Postal 1964 § 4.2.1, Ziff 1966, Katz and Martin 1967.

as having different underlying P-markers, which differ only in ways that are 'semantically insignificant'.[1] This can be accommodated by modifying the definition of 'intrinsic synonymy' so as to include pairs of expressions having the same underlying P-marker(s) or 'non-contrastive' P-markers.

The question of deciding which pairs of sentences stand in an active-passive relation may be compared to the question earlier discussed of determining M-relations. No difficulty arises when there is a clear formal correspondence, as in cases such as (3a) and (3b). But there may be instances which are more like the *go/went* problem, as e.g. if (3a) and

(3c) *Mary was bussed by John*

were grammatical, but (3b) and

(3d) **John bussed Mary*

were ungrammatical. Here *buss* could be treated as the 'passive of' *kiss*. If, however, we have a situation in which (3a), (3c) and (3d) are grammatical but (3b) ungrammatical, or (3a), (3b) and (3c) are grammatical but (3d) ungrammatical, the resolution of the choice between setting up one P-marker or two is less clear.[2]

It would of course be a complete confusion to appeal to the synonymity of *buss* and *kiss* as a 'reason' for settling the issue one way or the other. For their synonymity is assured whatever the solution. This is simply another way of putting the point that in grammatical analysis a synonymity statement about particular morphs may correspond either to the structural synonymity or to the intrinsic synonymity of pairs of sentences in which they occur, and this is here a relevant difference (whereas for purposes of phonological analysis it is irrelevant).

The relation of intrinsic synonymy is also, presumably, exemplified in cases of so-called 'symmetric predicates',[3] involving in

---

[1] Katz and Postal 1964, p. 73. Katz and Postal propose to treat passives as deriving from 'underlying P-markers containing an Adverb$_{manner}$ constituent dominating *by* plus a passive morpheme dummy' and not from the P-marker underlying the corresponding active (Katz and Postal 1964, p. 72). Cf. Katz and Martin 1967, p. 480, where 'sentences with the same underlying phrase marker or underlying phrase markers that are the same, except for elements that do not bear meaning' are said to be synonymous. The treatment proposed assumes that one of the 'semantic properties of dummy morphemes' is that they are assigned a null reading (Katz and Postal 1964, p. 73).

[2] There will doubtless be other considerations which weigh in favour of or against treating *buss* as an independent lexical item, e.g. whether or not we can say *There was a lot of bussing and cuddling at the party*.

[3] Langendoen 1969, pp. 94–95.

English the use of such verbs as *resemble*, *differ*, *marry*, *collide*:[1]

> *Tom resembles Dick*
> *Dick resembles Tom*
>
> *John's opinion differs from Bill's*
> *Bill's opinion differs from John's*
>
> *Peter is married to Joan*
> *Joan is married to Peter*
>
> *The car collided with the lorry*
> *The lorry collided with the car.*

That the difference between structural synonymy and intrinsic synonymy may relate to different dimensions of communicational relevance is suggested by the fact that there are many cases where one member of a pair of apparently intrinsically synonymous items rarely if ever occurs, and if it did occur would seem in some way odd or incongruous, e.g.

> *Paddington was left by the train at 4 o'clock precisely*
> (*The train left Paddington at 4 o'clock precisely*)
>
> *A haircut was had by John*
> (*John had a haircut*)
>
> *Strawberry jam is loved by Sheila*
> (*Sheila loves strawberry jam*).

Whereas it is difficult to find pairs of structurally but not intrinsically synonymous items which show a comparable disparity.

Both structural synonymy and intrinsic synonymy must be distinguished from 'analytic synonymy', which is a term we may reserve for describing part-to-part semantic correspondence of expressions which are, as wholes, synthetically synonymous. Thus to the extent that synonymous complex expressions are composed of semantically equivalent morphs and grammatical arrangements of morphs, we shall say they are analytically synonymous. The pairs cited previously

(1a) *He brought home some furze*
(1b) *He brought home some gorse*

and   (2a) *He wrapped the parcel up*
(2b) *He wrapped up the parcel*

---

[1] But not all English speakers use *collide* in this way, i.e. not all would regard *The car collided with a lamp post* as anomalous.

are analytically synonymous in this sense, the former pair being also structurally synonymous, and the latter pair intrinsically synonymous. Each morph and construction in (1a) can be matched with a semantically equivalent morph and construction in (1b), and similarly for (2a) and (2b). But

    (4a) *John likes his unmarried aunt*

and   (4b) *John likes his spinster aunt*

even if (let us assume)[1] structurally synonymous, are not analytically anonymous throughout in that *spinster* does not match *un+marri+ed*.

Where morphological analysis is concerned, the distinction between synthetic and analytic synonymy often answers to the difference between forms which are determinate with respect to segmentation and those which are not. Thus suppose we have a noun *zog* which has a regular plural by addition of *-s* and also an irregular plural without parallel elsewhere in the vocabulary; so that we say *one zog* but either *two zogs* or *two zigo*. Then *zogs* and *zigo* are synthetically synonymous but not analytically synonymous, since whereas the meaning of *zogs* can be treated as the meaning of *zog* plus the meaning 'more than one' of the suffix *-s*, the meaning of *zigo* is not comparably analysable in terms of the meanings of constituent parts. For in the case of morphs which are not determinate with respect to segmentation we cannot say what the constituent parts are.

Where syntactic analysis is concerned, analytic synonymity is a stronger condition of semantic equivalence than structural synonymity, as may be shown by comparing the requirements in terms of Katz and Postal's D5. That is to say, for two unambiguous sentences to be analytically synonymous it will have to be the case not only that they represent sentoids satisfying D5, but additionally that D5 hold for every corresponding pair of constituents dominated by C and C′ respectively, without residue, i.e. the pair of sentoids must match structurally in respect of occurrence of nodes. Thus in

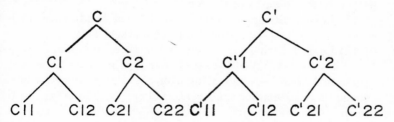

---

[1] Doubtless there is in fact a semantic difference, since John's unmarried aunt might be a young girl.

there will be structural synonymity if D5 is satisfied for C and C′, but analytic synonymity only if D5 holds for each of the pairs C and C′, C1 and C′1, C2 and C′2. Furthermore, the readings for the matching pairs of ultimate constituents C11 and C′11, C12 and C′12, C21 and C′21, C22 and C′22 must be the same. But the conditions cannot be satisfied for e.g.

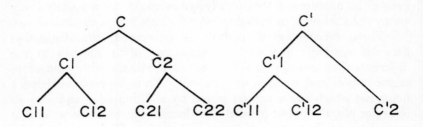

since C21 and C22 cannot be put in correspondence with anything under C′.

Accordingly C and C′ do not satisfy our requirement unless for any constituent (C1, C2...) immediately dominated by C there is a corresponding constituent (C′1, C′2...) immediately dominated by C′ such that the pairs of constituents (C1 and C′1, C2 and C′2,...) each satisfy D5, and similarly for constituents immediately dominated by those, until the ultimate constituents are reached.

The operation of a semantic component as outlined in Katz and Fodor 1963 and Katz and Postal 1964 would not normally allow for the distinction between synthetic and analytic synonymy to apply to sentences, since projection rules are cumulative, i.e. include an erasure proviso. Thus amalgamations of readings will be accomplished by a rule such as:

‘(R$_1$) Given two paths of the form

(1) Lexical String$_1$→syntactic markers of head→(a_1)→(a_2)→ ...→(a_n)→[1]<set of strings of markers Ω_1>

(2) Lexical String$_2$→syntactic markers of modifier →(b_1)→ (b_2)→...→(b_m)→[2]<set of strings of markers Ω_2>

such that there is a substring σ of the string of syntactic or semantic head markers and $\sigma\epsilon\Omega_2$. There is an amalgam of the form

Lexical String$_2$+Lexical String$_1$→ dominating node marker
→(a_1)→(a_2)→...→(a_n)→(b_1)→(b_2)→...→(b_m)→[[2] [1]]<Ω_1>
where any b_i is null when $(\exists a_i)$ $(b_i=a_i)$ and [[2] [1]] is [1] when
[2]=[1].'[1]

Katz and Fodor comment as follows:

'The limiting case, where the addition to the compound of
semantic material from the modifier is zero, is of considerable
theoretical significance. The compound *unmarried bachelor* is a case
in point. The erasure clause in (R_1), i.e., "any b_i is null when
$(\exists a_i)$ $(b_i=a_i)$ and [[2] [1]] is [1] when [2]=[1]," tells us to delete
from the path of the modifier any semantic material already represented in the path of the head. Thus, in forming the compound
unmarried bachelor all the semantic information in the path of the
modifier *unmarried* will be deleted so that the derived path for
unmarried bachelor will contain no more than the semantic material
which comes from the path for *bachelor*. The failure of the modifier
to add semantic information would appear to account for the intuition
that such expressions as *unmarried bachelor* are redundant and that,
correspondingly, such statements as "Bachelors are unmarried" are
empty, tautological, vacuous, uninformative.'[2]

Katz and Postal give a similar formulation for amalgamation by
projection rule[3] and defend it by asserting that 'it makes no sense to
include the semantic markers (Human) and (Female) twice in the
reading associated with the compound expression *spinster aunt* just
because each of the readings combined contains occurrences of both
these markers. In the derived reading for *spinster aunt* one occurrence
of these markers is sufficient; another occurrence of each adds no
semantic information.'[4]

What derived readings miss in this way is the fact that pairs like
spinster aunt and *unmarried aunt* are, if synonymous, synthetically
but not analytically synonymous. If we substitute for the first word
in *unmarried aunt* the word *spinster* we produce a phrase synthetically
synonymous with *unmarried aunt*; but we have not done it by
substituting a synonym for *unmarried*. This is indeed implicit in the
elimination of the 'redundant' semantic information by the projection
rule in the case of *spinster aunt*; but the derived reading no longer
distinguishes between various ways in which the 'nonredundant'

[1] Katz and Fodor 1963, p. 507.   [2] Katz and Fodor, 1963, p. 509.
[3] Katz and Postal 1964, p. 21.   [4] Katz and Postal 1964, p. 28, n. 10.

information represented by the reading has been accumulated.[1]
Thus all the synonymy definitions associated with the semantic
component are in effect definitions of synthetic synonymy.

It follows that differences between analytically and synthetically
synonymous constituents are not allowed to contribute to the derived
reading(s) of the sentences in which they occur. But this is a mistake.
For it takes no account of the distinction normally drawn by logicians
between two kinds of semantic equivalence. Analytic synonymy, as the
term has been used here, corresponds to what is sometimes called
'intensional isomorphism', or else appears as one of two possible
varieties of 'equivalence in analytic meaning'.

Carnap gives the following account of intensional isomorphism.

'Let us consider, as an example, the expressions '2+5' and 'II
sum V' in a language S containing numerical expressions and
arithmetical functors. Let us suppose that we see from the
semantical rules of S that both '+' and 'sum' are functors for
the function Sum and hence are L-equivalent; and, further, that
the numerical signs occurring have their ordinary meanings and
hence '2' and 'II' are L-equivalent to one another, and likewise
'5' and 'V'. Then we shall say that the two expressions are
intensionally isomorphic or that they have *the same intensional
structure*, because they not only are L-equivalent as a whole,
both being L-equivalent to '7', but consist of three parts in such

[1] It would, however, be misinterpreting the operation of the semantic component to object, as does McCawley, that that sentences with semantically anomalous
constituents turn out to be synonymous. According to McCawley: 'An assertion
that something anomalous is anomalous is a tautology and thus semantically impec-
cable, and there is nothing anomalous about reporting that someone has said
something anomalous. The latter facts are recognized by Katz who states (Katz
1965, p. 161): 'We may observe that the occurrence of a constituent without readings
is a necessary but *not* sufficient condition for a sentence to be semantically anomalous. For the sentence *We would think it queer indeed if someone were to say that he
smells itchy*, which contains a constituent without readings—which is semantically
anomalous—is not itself semantically anomalous'. However, the position that the
constituent in question has no readings is untenable, since that would mean that
    7. He says that he smells itchy.
    8. He says that he poured his mother into an inkwell.
    9. He says that his toenail sings five-part madrigals.
would be synonymous.' (McCawley 1968, pp. 128–129). But McCawley is wrong
since it does not follow that if two different constituents which violate selectional
restrictions are embedded in otherwise identical sentences then those sentences are
synonymous. What follows, on the contrary, is that such sentences will be meaningless, since the projection rules will give no combined reading for the node
labelled 'S'. The correct objection to Katz is just that. In other words, Katz by
his own theory is committed to a self-contradiction in claiming that there could be
a non-anomalous sentence which included a constituent with no reading. Katz is,
therefore, at fault, although not for the reason McCawley gives. (For an alternative
account of the semantics of such sentences as those cited, see Harris 1970).

a way that corresponding parts are L-equivalent to one another and hence have the same intension. Now it seems advisable to apply the concept of intensional isomorphism in a somewhat wider sense so that it holds also between expressions like '2+5' and 'sum (II, V)', because the use in the second expression of a functor preceding the two argument signs instead of one standing between them or of parentheses and a comma may be regarded as an inessential syntactic device. Analogously, if '>' and 'Gr' are L-equivalent, and likewise '3' and 'III', then we regard '5>3' as intensionally isomorphic to 'Gr (V, III)'. Here again we regard the two predicators '>' and 'Gr' as corresponding to each other, irrespective of their places in the sentences; further, we correlate the first argument expression of '>' with the first of 'Gr', and the second with the second. Further, '2+5>3' is isomorphic to 'Gr sum (II, V), III', because the corresponding expressions '2+5' and 'sum (II, V)' are not only L-equivalent but isomorphic. On the other hand, '7>3' and 'Gr sum (II, V), III' are not isomorphic; it is true that here again the two predicators '>' and 'Gr' are L-equivalent and that corresponding argument expressions of them are likewise L-equivalent, but the corresponding expressions '7' and 'sum (II, V)' are not isomorphic. We require for isomorphism of two expressions that the analysis of both down to the smallest subdesignators lead to analogous results.'[1]

Lewis specifies two conditions under which expressions are equivalent in analytic meaning: either

'(1) if at least one is elementary and they have the same intension, or (2) if, both being complex, they can be so analysed into constituents that (a) for every constituent in either, there is a corresponding constituent in the other which has the same intension, (b) no constituent distinguished in either has zero intension or universal intension, and (c) the order of corresponding constituents is the same in both, or can be made the same without alteration of the intension of either whole expression.[2]'

Condition (1) would include cases of synthetic synonymity, while condition (2) would include only cases of analytic synonymity.

The use which can be made of the distinction—as e.g. in Carnap's solution of Moore's paradox of analysis[3]—affords ample evidence of its importance, and at the same time of the inadequacy of the trans-

---

[1] Carnap 1947, § 14.1.   [2] Lewis 1944, p. 246.   [3] Carnap 1947, § 15.1.

formationalist's concept of 'synonymy' (='synthetic synonymy'.)
For the transformationalist who operates with a semantic component
as described by Katz, Fodor and Postal must say that the sentences
    (6) *A brother is a brother*
and   (7) *A brother is a male sibling*
although having different P-markers are 'fully synonymous' (are 'full
paraphrases'), and he is thus unable to explain how it is that these
sentences have different communicational uses, and in particular
how it is that (6) is totally uninformative whereas (7) is not. This
difference cannot be attributed to the difference in form between (6)
and (7), and must therefore be attributable to a difference between
the meanings of the sentences. Yet, according to the transformationalist's account, there will be no difference between the meanings of
the sentences.

Such examples point clearly to the need for distinguishing
between two quite different implications of synonymity statements
in a way which is, again, irrelevant at the level of phonological
analysis.

The notion of 'intrinsic synonymy' raises the question of how,
ultimately, a distinction is to be drawn between items which just
'happen' to be synonymous, and those whose surface synonymity
reflects an underlying identity at some more abstract level; as e.g.
when we consider why one should treat pairs like
    John kissed Mary
and   *Mary was kissed by John*
as coming from the same or noncontrastive P-markers, but not pairs
like
    John pleased Mary
and   *Mary liked John.*
It may be—and has been—regarded as a defect in Chomskyite
transformational grammar that pairs of the latter type are not treated
as transformationally related in a way that derives them from a
common deep structure. Both pairs appear to be synthetically
synonymous, and in a way which is systematically related to the
synonymity of many parallel pairs of sentences in English.

A proposal which merits consideration in the present context is
the following:
A3 In *axy* and *bxy*, *a* and *b* are synonymous if whatever difference

in meaning there may be between *axy* and *bxy* is entirely determined by a difference in relations between deep and surface structure of *axy* and *bxy*.

Thus, for example, if *a* and *b* are verbs, and the semantic difference between *axy* and *bxy* resides in the fact that the 'logical subject' of *axy* is also the 'grammatical subject' of the sentence, whereas the 'logical subject' of *bxy* is not, then it becomes possible to regard that difference as automatically determining the choice between *a* and *b* if *a* and *b* make no other independent contributions to the meanings of *axy* and *bxy*, and if these deep structure/surface structure relations are characteristic for sentences containing *a* and *b*.

In Fillmore's elaboration of the theory of case grammar, it is proposed to treat the relations between various pairs of verbs as under A3. Each sentence is envisaged as having a 'case frame' which specifies the 'array of cases' the sentence provides. Case frames are represented in square brackets, with 'underline' indicating the position of the element with respect to which the expression is an environmental frame; e.g. the frame [___A] is one into which the verb *run* may be inserted, 'A' standing for the Agentive case and specifying the requirement of a 'typically animate perceived instigator of the action identified by the verb'.[1] Verbs are envisaged as having in their lexical entries 'frame features' which indicate the set of case frames into which the verb in question may be inserted. Frame features are represented in square brackets with '+' or '−' in front, indicating that the set of case frames represented by the expression within the brackets is that which will (if the feature is marked '+') or which will not (if the feature is marked '−') accept the lexical item in question. Parentheses indicate optional choices, and linked parentheses the obligatory inclusion of at least one of the elements so linked. Thus the verb *kill* has the frame feature '+[___D(I)(A)]' specifying the requirement of 'an animate being affected by the state or action identified by the verb', and either an 'inanimate force or object causally involved in the action or state identified by the verb', or a 'typically animate perceived instigator of the action identified by the verb', or both. Verbs are regarded as being distinguished one from another not only in respect of the case frames into which they can be inserted, but also in respect of their transformational properties, including the selection of particular NPs to become surface subject or surface object of the verb.

---

[1] Fillmore 1968, pp. 24–25. Other cases are: Instrumental ('I'), Dative ('D'), Factitive ('F'), Locative ('L') and Objective ('O').

When sentences are analysed in this way, it is feasible to show, according to Fillmore, 'that some syntactically different words are in fact semantically identical (with respect to that aspect of their meanings which is independent of the contribution of the associated cases).' Thus *like* and *please* 'may be described as being synonymous. Each has the frame feature +[＿＿O+D]; they differ only in their subject selection features. The verb *like*, in fact, has in its history the subject selection feature possessed by *please*.'[1]

On this basis, a classification of lexical items may be drawn up, depending on the various possible ways in which synonymy combines with variation of frame features and other grammatical differentiae. *Like* and *please* will belong to the class of synonyms showing identical frame features. *Show* and *see*, on the other hand, will be synonyms which contrast in presence vs. absence of a particular case category in their frame features (*show*= +[＿＿O+D+A] vs. *see*= +[＿＿ O+D]). Whereas *see* and *look* will be synonyms which contrast in the substitution of one case category for another in their respective frame features (*see*= +[＿＿O+D] vs. *look*= +[＿＿O+A]).[2]

An analysis on basically similar lines (although without the specific case grammar framework) is involved in Lyons's proposals to treat *kill* and *die* as 'alternative, syntactically-conditioned, phonological realizations of the 'same' verb',[3] or, more specifically, to treat *kill* as 'the 'lexicalized' two-place causative form of *die*', and likewise French *montrer* as 'the 'lexicalized' three-place causative of *voir*'.[4] Lyons suggests that the deep-structure descriptions of sentences will employ such labels as '+ ag' (=Agentive) and '+

---

[1] Fillmore 1968, p. 30. According to Moore, the situation is somewhat more complicated than Fillmore allows for. Citing the examples
    (1c) *I liked the play*
    (1d) *The play pleased me*
    (6a) *The children pleased Sue yesterday by making their beds*
    (6b) *Sue liked the children yesterday for making their beds*
Moore observes: 'I believe (6a) is ambiguous between the reading that *Sue* was pleased by *the children* where *the children* are in the same case relation, OBJECT, to *Sue* as, in (1d), *play* is to *me* and on the other hand the reading that *the children* are not in the case relation dominating *the play*, but are dominated by AGENT and thus are assigned the reading: animate responsible source of the action identified by the verb. Evidence that (6a) is indeed ambiguous is provided by sentences such as
    the children set out to please Sue
    the children set out to like Sue
where the first, but not the second, seems a clear case of an ordinary sentence needing no special interpretation. This much additional evidence suggests that *please* requires in its case frame the contextual feature +[＿＿OA] with the further constraint that the OBJECT selected must be [+ human], an object selection feature that does not apply to *like*' (Moore 1970).
   [2] Fillmore 1968, pp. 30–31.   [3] Lyons 1968, § 8.2.4.   [4] Lyons 1968, § 8.2.14.

caus' (=Causative), and that the lexicon should contain e.g. such information under *soft* as will permit '*soft*: + caus' to be realized as *soften*.[1]

Fillmore's proposals amount in effect to modifying the scope of the concept 'synonymy' in a way which may be quite simply related to earlier proposals[2] in generative grammar as follows (ignoring possible differences of opinion about the interpretation of particular examples).

Under the definition of synonymy whereby

(D5) C and C' are *fully synonymous with respect to PM and PM'* if and only if the set of readings associated with the node labeled 'C' in PM and the set of readings associated with the node labeled 'C'' in PM' are identical; PM may equal PM'.[3]

it emerges that in the case of constituents consisting of single items listed in the lexicon, two such items must have identical lexical entries in order to qualify as full synonyms. For only on that condition will the readings in question, i.e. the paths comprising a complete sequence of symbols for syntactic marker(s), semantic marker(s), distinguisher (if any) and selection restriction(s), be identical.

Let us now introduce the term 'S-reading' to refer to that section of a path in a lexical entry excluding syntactic markers and selection restrictions, i.e. that part of the path comprising only a subsequence of semantic marker(s) and distinguisher if any.

We may now define 'nuclear equivalents' as lexical items which do not differ in respect of their S-readings.

The suggestions made by Fillmore concerning the relation between the pairs *like* and *please*, *show* and *see* etc. amount to extending the term 'synonymy' to cover cases of nuclear equivalence in instances such as these, together with a concomitant proposal about the deep-structure syntactic characterization of lexical items by reference to cases, this new method of characterization allowing us to restrict the information required in the S-reading in various ways.

The question may now be put: 'What is there to choose between a concept of synonymy which admits nuclear equivalence as a

[1] Lyons 1968, § 8.3.6.
[2] E.g. Katz and Fodor 1963, Katz and Postal 1964.
[3] Katz and Postal 1964, p. 27.

sufficient condition of the synonymity of lexical items (in at least some cases) and one which does not?'

What is ultimately at issue here is the validity of rival views of the boundary between semantics and grammar. In order to count different lexical items as synonymous, we must be able to show that any apparent semantic difference between them is in fact 'merely grammatical' and thus can plausibly be accounted for at the grammatical level, leaving the items in question to be characterized as identical at the semantic level.

Fillmore is open to the criticism of failure to provide this justification, and the criticism is not that he has omitted to do so, but that his position affords no possible basis for doing so. It is true that Fillmore has shown how to describe certain similarities and differences between words by employing a grammatical terminology ('Agentive', 'Dative', 'subject selection' etc.); but it would be naive to suppose that it followed from the correctness and consistency of such descriptions that the facts described were grammatical facts.

The reason why e.g. *like* and *please* cannot be regarded as synonyms which happen to differ in 'subject selection' is the same as the reason why *king* and *queen* cannot be regarded as synonyms which happen to differ in 'gender'; namely, that no amount of grammatical description or re-description will reduce the semantic difference. Particular grammatical and semantic facts may be closely interrelated: that does not mean that there is a class of facts with regard to which it is an arbitrary choice, or one of convenience, whether we say they are part of the speaker's grammatical knowledge, or part of his semantic knowledge. And even if there were such a 'borderline' class, the facts about *like* and *please* have no stronger claim to be put in it than the facts about *king* and *queen*. It is, for example, quite clearly a grammatical fact about *king* and *queen* that either can be substituted for the other *salva grammaticalitate* in the sentence frame

The——lived in a palace.

To call it also a grammatical fact that the substitution cannot be effected *salva significatione* would make nonsense of any distinction between grammatical and semantic knowledge. (It would simply leave us to find new terms for a distinction between two essentially different types of 'grammatical' knowledge.)

Similarly, it is a grammatical fact about *like* and *please* that either can be substituted for the other *salva grammaticalitate* in the sentence frame

John——s Mary.

Equally, it is a semantic fact that the substitution cannot be effected *salva significatione*. But to say this is to say that there is a semantic difference between them. And to say that there is a semantic difference between two expressions is to deny their synonymity.

CHAPTER FOUR

Synonymy and semantic analysis

In semantic analysis questions of synonymy arise in connexion with establishing the general (i.e. language-neutral) conditions governing criteria for relational characterizations of a certain kind in semantic descriptions. A semantic description is here taken to be an account of the semantic knowledge shared by the participants in communication situations. In the case of a natural language, we postulate semantic knowledge in order to account for certain features of communication between language-users. In the case of a constructed language, the specification of semantic knowledge serves to delimit possibilities of communication between language-users. In either case, there must be procedures for determining whether given expressions are in fact used in accordance with given semantic characterizations. These are the procedures which, in the case of a natural language, would be appealed to in order to support a correct characterization or to refute an erroneous one.

There are two types of semantic characterization we are particularly concerned with, and these may be represented as follows:

ρ1. '$a=b$'
ρ2. '$a \neq b$'.

A characterization of the former type tells us that expression a and expression b do not differ semantically, while a characterization of the latter type tells us that expression a differs semantically (in some unspecified respect) from expression b. It is proposed to explicate the notion of a synonymity statement for purposes of semantic analysis—i.e. to answer the question 'What is it to say of two expressions of L that they are (or are not) synonymous?'—by reference to characterizations of the above types. We shall examine how such a statement might be justified for any pair of expressions a and b in a language L. To do this, it will be necessary to consider how ρ-characterizations are related to characterizations of a different kind.

It is clear that a semantic description of L which provided *only* semantic characterizations of type 'ρ1' and type 'ρ2' would be incomplete in the obvious sense that, while telling us whether any expression of L did or did not differ semantically from any other expression of L, it would fail to tell us in what way any two semantically differing expressions differed. It would thus fall short of an adequate account of a competent speaker's semantic knowledge of those expressions. For example, a semantic description of English which includes the following $\rho2$ characterization

'*rhinoceros* $\neq$ *dibatag*'

tells us that the words *rhinoceros* and *dibatag* differ semantically. But in order to discover how they differ we should need to have available semantic characterizations of a different type from '$\rho2$', for example

'*rhinoceros*: quadruped with horned nose. . . .'

'*dibatag*: long-necked antelope. . . .'

Characterizations like these will be termed 'σ-characterizations' or 'substantive semantic characterizations' and represented as

'a: α . . . .'

'b: β . . . .' etc.,

to distinguish them from the 'relational semantic characterizations' of type '$\rho1$' and type '$\rho2$'. These typographical conventions correspond to the fact that 'a', 'b' etc. are expressions of the object-language (or language under description), while 'α', 'β' etc. are expressions of the metalanguage (or language of description).

We may distinguish between a stronger and a weaker condition to be imposed on semantic characterizations. In the case of σ-characterizations, the weaker condition is met if the metalinguistic description states a meaning for the given expression, but without indicating the semantic structure of the expression, i.e. without analysing the expression into its meaning-bearing elements, or stating how a composite meaning for the whole is provided by the arrangement of these elements. For example, the characterization 'sour apple' for an expression e does not in itself indicate e.g. whether or not there is one part of e which means 'sour' and another part of e which means 'apple', and another part, or feature of arrangement, of e which combines these two meanings in the way indicated by the meta-linguistic expression 'sour apple'. The stronger condition for σ-characterizations is that they should provide precisely such an analysis. We may term characterizations which meet only the weaker condition 'synthetic characterizations', and those which meet the stronger 'analytic characterizations'.

In keeping with the distinction earlier drawn between synthetic and analytic synonymy, we may likewise distinguish between synthetic and analytic ρ-characterizations, the former indicating only whether two expressions do or do not differ semantically as wholes, and the latter whether or not they differ semantically in respect of their internal structure.

For notational convenience, we may distinguish when necessary by prefixing 'S' in the case of synthetic, and 'A' in the case of analytic characterizations ($S\sigma$, $A\sigma$, $S\rho1$, $A\rho1$, $S\rho2$, $A\rho2$). When that distinction is irrelevant to the discussion, the prefixed letter may be omitted.

In this way it is possible to treat a semantic description[1] as a store of information organized so as to produce when required σ-characterizations and ρ-characterizations; that is, for any given expression the description will provide a sequence of metalinguistic symbols (its σ-characterization) formulating the competent speaker's semantic knowledge of that expression, and for any given pair of expressions the description provides a metalinguistic symbolization (ρ-characterization) expressing their semantic equivalence or non-equivalence. Such a description, if exhaustive, gives a complete account of the semantic knowledge of a speaker of L in the sense of including the information that would be given by a complete inventory of the expressions of L with their substantive semantic characterizations. It will tell us not merely that expressions of L differ semantically, but in detail how they differ semantically. Although a complete inventory, i.e. list, cannot be drawn up if L is a natural language, because of the indefinitely large number of sentences in any natural language, the information available will nonetheless enable us to find the appropriate substantive semantic characterization for any desired sentence. By the same token, a complete list of synonymous expressions cannot be drawn up: the most we can hope for if L is a natural language is to be able to determine for any desired pair of expressions

---

[1] Explicit proposals for systematizing semantic descriptions are discussed in Katz and Fodor 1963, Katz and Postal 1964, Weinreich 1966, Katz 1967a, and elsewhere. Such systematizations are not our present concern. Since the issues to be discussed in the present chapter arise independently of any specific proposals as to the best means of arranging the information in a semantic description, it will be preferable to continue to treat semantic characterizations in the abstract way exemplified above. For our interest here is in the content of a characterization, not in how that content ought to be represented, broken down, and related to other characterizations by means of devices such as projection rules, semantic markers etc. Furthermore, confinement to a systematization of the kind currently accepted in work on the semantic component of a generative grammar is unacceptable, since that model embodies presupposition of the semantic determinacy of expressions, a position which is not well established (see below, and Bolinger 1965, p. 571).

whether or not their substantive semantic characterizations are the same.

This completes our account of the minimum conceptual apparatus required to tackle synonymy as a problem of semantic description. The next step is an inquiry into the justification of ρ-characterizations.

We may approach the question of the relationship between relational characterizations (ρ-characterizations) and substantive characterizations (σ-characterizations) by supposing first of all that we have available a completed semantic description of L, and postulating that it is organized in such a way that the ρ-characterization for a and b expresses the identity or non-identity of whatever σ-characterizations are assigned to a and b. On this assumption, relational characterizations of type '$\rho 1$' are abbreviated statements to the effect that a and b have the same σ-characterization, while relational characterizations of type '$\rho 2$' are abbreviated statements to the effect that a and b do not have the same σ-characterization. We may term a semantic description of L which gives both relational and substantive characterizations an 'internally consistent' description if for any a and any b a ρ-characterization '$a=b$' appears if and only if a and b have the same σ-characterization, and a ρ-characterization '$a \neq b$' appears if and only if a and b do not have the same σ-characterization. In the case of synthetic σ-characterizations there will be a corresponding synthetic ρ-characterization (of type $S\rho 1$ or $S\rho 2$), while in the case of analytic σ-characterizations there will be a corresponding analytic ρ-characterization (of type $A\rho 1$ or $A\rho 2$).

A criterion has now been formulated by which the internal consistency of semantic descriptions may be judged. Obviously, however, a particular semantic description of L might easily pass the criterion of internal consistency, yet be wrong in the sense of giving an erroneous account of the semantic facts. For example, a semantic description of English which contained the ρ-characterization

'*rhinoceros=dibatag*'

and the σ-characterizations

'*rhinoceros*: quadruped with horned nose. . . .'

and   '*dibatag*: quadruped with horned nose. . . .'

would be (in this respect) an internally consistent description, but it would be wrong in view of the fact (granted that it is a fact) that for speakers of English the words *rhinoceros* and *dibatag* are not semantically identical, and specifically in view of the fact that 'quadruped with horned nose . . . .' (granted the usual sense of these words in English, here taken to be the metalanguage) is not a correct semantic character-ization of *dibatag*.

It follows that we cannot adequately characterize that semantic knowledge which is knowledge of synonymy in terms of the structure of a description of *L*, since the strongest guarantee of synonymy this account gives is one of internal consistency of the semantic description of *L*. But because it is possible to construct an internally consistent description which could be wrong about instances of synonymity, there would be no way of deciding which of two different but internally consistent semantic descriptions of *L* correctly represented the knowledge of synonymy of speakers of *L*.

The difference between two rival semantic descriptions need not involve gross incompatibilities (as between a description of English which included the ρ-characterization '*rhinoceros=dibatag*' and a description of English which included the ρ-characterization '*rhinoceros ≠ dibatag*'). It might be the case that description 'A' draws more or different semantic distinctions as compared with description 'B', with the result that expressions which are characterized as semantically equivalent under one description are characterized as showing a slight semantic difference under the other.[1] Thus we should have two rather different accounts of the speakers' knowledge of synonymy; but again the question which account was to be preferred could not be settled by reference to the internal structure of the descriptions concerned.

The reason why proposals in semantics which afford no basis for external criteria of synonymy (i.e. criteria which go outside the structure of the semantic description) lack the means of deciding questions about the correctness of ρ-characterizations is that they leave unclear which facets of the speaker's semantic knowledge are to be understood as corresponding to the concept 'synonymy'. For example, in 'The structure of a semantic theory' Katz and Fodor speak of 'the ability to interpret sentences', and distinguish various aspects of this ability:

> 'The speaker's exercise of this ability . . . provides empirical data for the construction of a semantic theory, just as the construction of a grammar draws upon empirical data supplied by the exercise of the speaker's ability to distinguish well-

---

[1] This situation is found in dictionaries which purport to be dictionaries of the same natural language. One dictionary draws a distinction between two words which another dictionary glosses identically.

formed sentences from ungrammatical strings, to recognize
syntactic ambiguity, and to appreciate relations between
sentence types. A semantic theory describes and explains the
interpretative ability of speakers: by accounting for their per-
formance in determining the number and content of the readings
of a sentence; by detecting semantic anomalies; by deciding
upon paraphrase relations between sentences; and by marking
every other semantic property or relation that plays a role in this
ability.'[1]

This formulation could perhaps serve as a model for drafting a
preliminary statement about that aspect of the speaker's semantic
knowledge which corresponds to the concept 'synonymy'. If for
'ability to interpret sentences' one substitutes 'ability to interpret
expressions', then we could suppose that the speaker has the ability
to place every pair of different expressions in the language into one
or other of two classes, according to whether members of a given pair
do or do not receive the same interpretation. Knowledge of synonymy
would thus correspond to that part of interpretative ability which
informs the speaker's judgments of interpretational 'sameness' and
'difference'.

   But this takes us only as far as the notion of 'ρ-characterization'
already discussed. For talk of the speaker's ability to put pairs of
expressions into classes cannot be taken as indicating a type of
informant test criterial for determining instances of synonymity.
Until further progress can be made towards stating what typical skills
flow from knowledge of synonymy, no more has been done than to
draw a tentative and quite general distinction within a certain area of
linguistic knowledge. (It is as if one had said, for example, that it is
to be supposed that part of having normal vision is being able to
detect similarities and differences of colour: doubtless true, but no
more than a point of departure and, as the statement of an explic-
andum, a vague one at that.)

   The clarification supplied in 'The structure of a semantic theory'
is hardly satisfactory. A distinction appears to be drawn between
two types of case where a language might have expressions differing
in form but identical in meaning, the term 'synonymy' being
restricted to expressions which constitute individual lexical items in
the dictionary, and the term 'paraphrase' being applied to expressions
which constitute sentences of the language. No account is given of

---

[1] Katz and Fodor 1963, p. 486.

H

communicational skills which correspond to knowledge of synonyms; but there is an account of 'paraphrasing skill'. The communication situation imagined is that of speakers of English receiving an anonymous letter containing only the English sentence '*S*'. Their ability to interpret '*S*' is contrasted with that of 'persons who do not speak English, but are equipped with a completely adequate grammar of English'. 'Paraphrasing skill' is listed among the abilities of the speakers of English, and described in the following terms:

> 'Finally, whatever sentence the anonymous letter contains, as a rule, speakers of English can easily decide what sentences are paraphrases of it and what are not in the sense that they can answer such questions as: what does the letter say? does the letter say such-and-such? how can what the letter says be rephrased? This facet of the speaker's ability cannot be referred to his mastery of grammar either, for the group who are equipped with a grammar but who do not speak English will be unable to tell whether or not a sentence is a paraphrase of *S*. The reasons are simply that there need be no definite grammatical relation between a sentence and its paraphrases; e.g. "Two chairs are in the room" and "There are at least two things in the room and each is a chair"; and that where a definite grammatical relation obtains between a pair of sentences, neither need be a paraphrase of the other, e.g. "The ball was hit by the man" and "The ball was hit", "The man hit the ball", and "The man did not hit the ball". Thus, still another facet of the speaker's semantic ability which must fall within the domain of a semantic theory in his paraphrasing skill.'[1]

This account invites, if it does not involve, a serious confusion between speech acts (e.g. those comprising a letter) and sentences. 'What does the letter say?' is a question about speech acts, and so are the other questions put to the two imaginary groups of 'informants'. It thus appears that the Katz-Fodor account of paraphrasing skill is based on a latent theory of speech acts; but this theory is never made explicit, still less justified. Insofar as one can reconstruct it from the somewhat scanty remarks in 'The structure of a semantic theory', it appears to involve at least the following thesis:

> (All?) sentences in *L* can be grouped into pairs (e.g. 'S1' and 'S2') or larger sets ('S1', 'S2', 'S3' . . .) of *paraphrases*, between which certain (so far unspecified) semantic relations hold. A

---

[1] Katz and Fodor 1963, pp. 493-4.

speech act which is a question about the purport of another (any other?) speech act involving the utterance of 'Sx' can be correctly (and fully?) answered if (and only if?) the answerer knows whether some other sentence 'Sy' is a paraphrase of 'Sx'.

But if this partial reconstruction of the speech act theory underlying 'The structure of a semantic theory' is in essentials correct, it becomes evident that the only account given of 'paraphrasing skill' is a circular one. That is to say, 'paraphrasing skill' is presented as (part of) the knowledge which enables the speaker to perform successfully certain speech acts, the speech acts in question being those which manifest a knowledge of paraphrases. This circularity is further evident in Katz and Fodor's comments on projection rules, e.g. it is asserted that the semantic interpretation assigned by the projection rules must 'account . . . for the speaker's ability to understand sentences' by, *inter alia*, suitably relating 'sentences speakers know to be paraphrases of each other'.[1] In other words, the rules must account for paraphrasing skill by marking paraphrases as paraphrases.

This leaves an explanatory gap in 'The structure of a semantic theory', a gap which is not—and could not be—filled by occasional exemplification: i.e. it is of no avail to say that a speaker lacks 'paraphrasing skill' if he does not know that e.g. *There are at least two things in the room and each is a chair* is a paraphrase of *Two chairs are in the room.* For this is merely to agree to call a certain pair of sentences 'paraphrases', i.e. we here explain 'paraphrasing skill' as knowledge that e.g. *a* and *b* 'are paraphrases'. But what one wants to know is not what to call such sentences, but just what it means to call them 'paraphrases'.[2]

There might be two possible explanations of this lacuna in 'The

---

[1] Katz and Fodor 1963, pp. 493–4.

[2] A similar objection may be brought against the use of the term 'paraphrase' by Southworth, who proposes 'that we consider as basic linguistic data the information that certain parts of a corpus are paraphrases of each other' (Southworth 1967, p. 345). In Southworth's case the objection is particularly crucial, since 'paraphrase' is a key term. Southworth's claim is that paraphrase is one of the two 'inter-sentence relations' to which all others can be reduced. But it is not at all clear what Southworth means when he calls certain sentences of English 'paraphrases'. E.g. *The committee rejected the proposal unanimously* is said to have as 'paraphrases' both *The committee's rejection of the proposal was unanimous* and *Each of the committee members rejected the proposal.* But it seems at least contentious that the truth conditions for these three sentences are identical, and thus in doubt whether they have the same meaning. Southworth's comment that to call two sentences 'paraphrases' is not the same as saying that they 'mean the same' is hardly illuminating, and apart from examples the only explanation of his claim is, unfortunately, a definition which relies on a prior notion (that of 'implication') which stands in just as much need of clarification.

structure of a semantic theory'. One would be that 'paraphrase' is not defined because there is already an established and generally accepted theory of paraphrases, too well known to need explicit recapitulation. But this cannot be the explanation because in 1963, when Katz and Fodor's paper was first published, there was no such theory. The other explanation would be the 'we-all-know-(roughly)-what-is-meant-by-'x'' explanation. But this is an explanation which will not do at all here. Insofar as we do know (roughly) what is meant by Katz and Fodor's 'paraphrase', it is because we have read other (equally vague) grammatical and philosophical writings where that term is employed, not because we know as a matter of experience as language-users that there 'are paraphrases', that paraphrases 'really exist'. (The case is analogous to that of 'sense datum'. The term 'sense datum' gets its sense from its (somewhat controversial) role in discussions of the philosophy of perception, not from our observations of people (including ourselves) engaged in perceiving. Accordingly, it would be quite question-begging to impose as an empirical constraint on a theory of perception that it account correctly for sense-data.) Of course, doubtless speakers do, in particular situations, react to the utterance of different sentences in ways which are in certain respects similar. But in order to clarify the concept 'paraphrase', what needs to be made clear is which of these similarities, or which aspects of these similarities, are under discussion when the term 'paraphrase' is used.

The question then arises: what is the point of imposing upon a semantic theory—or upon any theory, for that matter—an empirical condition of adequacy 'K' (in this case 'K' is 'correct account of paraphrasing skill') prior to a definition of the terms used in stating 'K'?

The answer is: none. And the obvious explanation for the appearance of such a condition in 'The structure of a semantic theory' is simply that the alleged semantic skills have been invented in advance to provide explanatory functions suited to the capacity of the model which its authors are about to propose for the semantic component of a linguistic description.

To say this, it should be noted, is not to deny the utility of the model: it is simply to advocate dropping the pretence that 'K' states an empirical constraint.

One further general point should be made concerning the correlation of descriptions to describienda. One might agree with someone who maintained that an important requirement for road-maps was that B-roads should be marked as B-roads. Agreement with such a person is not entirely vacuous inasmuch as there might be others who maintained the (surprising) thesis that B-roads should be marked as A-roads or others again who maintained that B-roads should never be marked at all. Thus agreeing with Katz and Fodor that paraphrases should be marked as paraphrases is to cast a vote against e.g. such proposals as that paraphrases should be marked as semantically anomalous, or that paraphrases should not be indicated at all. But the theorist of map-making may have a critic who maintains that, since a map purports to provide correct information about roads, unless there is an agreed definition of what counts as a B-road it may be misleading for a map to distinguish between B-roads and others. The same critic might also point out that, in the absence of such a definition, it is difficult to know exactly what insistence on the principle of marking B-roads as B-roads amounts to. To such a critic our theorist of map-making might perhaps reply: 'Everybody knows what a B-road is. In any case, if there is someone who doesn't, then he should not look to me to supply a definition, because it is not my job.' (One would then form an appropriate view of his claim to be a theorist of map-making.) But it would be even sillier of him to reply: 'Oh, but a map constructed according to my principles tells you which the B-roads are. The map itself supplies the definition.' If our theorist replied in this latter sense, he would have missed the point of the question, and have given a circular answer into the bargain. Anyone who supposed that 'The structure of a semantic theory' offered a means of defining 'paraphrase' for any language described according to the principles there advocated would be involved in an exactly analogous circularity.

The conclusion argued for thus far has been the purely negative one that an adequate account of knowledge of synonymy cannot be provided in terms of the structure of the semantic description itself. Consideration will now be given to a more positive specification of the requirements, i.e. we shall inquire what constraints external to the structure of the semantic description of L affect setting up ρ-characterizations. We shall first consider certain constraints which follow from the basic reasons for the explanatory postulation of semantic knowledge. Here there arises the question of how linguistic knowledge is connected with pragmatic judgments arising out of communication (e.g. judging whether what someone says is true, what the correct answer to someone's question is, etc.), such judgments presupposing the prior correct interpretation of words used in speech acts. We shall be particularly concerned with the connexions between the meanings of sentences and the possibility of using sentences to make true or false statements.

Semantic knowledge is postulated—on the view we are here taking—in order to account for the possibility of communicational exchanges, including the exchange of information about extra-linguistic facts. But, for epistemological reasons, acquiring knowledge of the truth of p cannot be equated with understanding a verbal expression in which the statement p is formulated. Otherwise, to cite Frege's example,[1] it could have been known without the help of astronomical observation that the sentence *The Morning Star is (the same as) the Evening Star* expressed a true statement. By the same token, we are led to distinguish meaning from reference.[2] For if an identity statement expressed by a sentence of the form 'a is b' is true, then it must be the case that one and the same item X is referred to both by the expression a and by the expression b. But if to understand the expression a were no more and no less than to know that X is referred to by a, and to understand the expression b were likewise to know that X is referred to by b, then anyone who understood the sentence 'a is b' would also know the truth of the identity statement.

The argument from identity statements enables us to make some progress towards identifying the skills which flow from knowledge of synonymy, for it makes apparent one constraint upon setting up p-characterizations, if the latter are to serve the purpose of representing knowledge of synonymy.

Consider a proposed semantic description Sd of a language La in which a and b are proper names having the same bearer.[3] Let us

---

[1] Frege 1892.

[2] In Frege's terminology, *Sinn* from *Bedeutung*. But there are reasons for questioning the usual translation of Frege's *Bedeutung* by *reference* (Tugendhat 1970).

[3] It is sometimes held that proper names 'have no meaning' (for a criticism of this doctrine, see Sørensen 1963 Ch. 4), and it might therefore be questioned whether proper names fall within the scope of a theory of synonymy. The supposition underlying the present discussion is that a semantic description assigns a σ-characterization to any expressions whose interchange systematically affects the content of speech acts. Thus if English speakers use e.g. *Is this the road to Edinburgh?* to ask a different question from *Is this the road to London?*, and likewise *I live in Edinburgh* to make a different statement from *I live in London*, etc. then the proper names *Edinburgh* and *London* are assigned σ-characterizations in a semantic description of English. The view that proper names have meanings is argued for in Frege 1891. Cf. also Searle 1958.

suppose that *Sd* gives the following σ-characterizations:

'*a*: proper name of Σ'

'*b*: proper name of Σ'

(where 'Σ' is an individual constant in the metalanguage). It follows that if *Sd* is an internally consistent description by the criterion previously proposed, *Sd* gives also the ρ-characterization:

'*a=b*'.

But here the σ-characterizations represent the fact that speakers of *La* know the identity of reference of *a* and *b*, which, if we accept the argument from identity statements, cannot be equated with knowing that *a* and *b* have the same meaning. Thus if we wish our ρ-characterizations to indicate synonymities, we are led to stipulate a prohibition on setting up relational characterizations of type '$\rho1$' in any instance where the relevant σ-characterizations merely supply an individual constant identifying the bearer of a name.

It should be noted that this prohibition also sets a condition on the completeness of semantic descriptions. This is evident when we consider the result of applying the prohibition to *Sd*. Let us call the semantic description so modified '*Sdi*'. In *Sdi* we are debarred from setting up the ρ-characterization '*a=b*'. Should we, then, set up the '$\rho2$' characterization '$a \neq b$'? But this is not allowed either, for such characterizations are—so far—set up if and only if the relevant σ-characterizations differ, and in this case they do not differ. Thus we have a pair of expressions of the same semantic type (proper names), for which *Sdi* fails to provide any ρ-characterization at all. It follows that *Sdi* cannot be a complete description of *La*.

An exactly parallel case can be constructed substituting for the proper names *a* and *b* in *La* two referring expressions which are not proper names. In this way the argument is generalized from proper names to referring expressions of all kinds, and an exactly parallel prohibition on setting up ρ-characterizations must be extended to all referring expressions. Thus if the σ-characterizations for referring expressions in *La* merely supply individual constants of the metalanguage identifying the referents of those expressions, no corresponding ρ-characterizations can be set up, and it must be concluded that the semantic description is incomplete. Such a conclusion is obviously correct, the missing element in the semantic description being a representation of the knowledge which might enable users of *La* to understand sentences formulating identity statements without *ipso facto* knowing the truth or falsity of the statements in question.

Frege's argument from identity statements may be developed further to throw some light on synonymy of referring expressions. For if it is accepted that astronomical observation is required to determine whether or not a statement formulated as *The Morning Star is the Evening Star* is true, it is thereby implied that semantic knowledge is inadequate to settle that question, i.e. that the truth in question is not an analytic truth, and the sentence in question not an analytic sentence.[1] But if this is so, however the meanings of the expressions *the Morning Star* and *the Evening Star* be defined, it is at least clear that these expressions are not synonymous referring expressions. For if they were, then the truth of the identity statement would be assured without reliance on astronomers, since to question it would be to question the truth of a tautology which might be alternatively formulated as *The Morning Star is the Morning Star*.

This conclusion assumes: (i) that we are not dealing with 'referentially ambiguous' expressions,[2] (ii) that we are concerned with a conceptual system in which the denial that X is X is self-contradictory, and (iii) that the copula sentence is 'semantically endocentric' with respect to the referring expressions occurring in it, i.e. that this is a case where 'the meaning of a sentence is a function of the terms which occur in the sentence.'[3]

We may for purposes of the present discussion define 'semantic endocentricity' as follows. Any expression is semantically endocentric with respect to its parts if and only if the meaning assigned to it is exclusively determined by the meanings of the parts and of their combination.[4]

---

[1] We may define an analytic truth as one belonging to a certain conceptual system within which its denial is self-contradictory. It is thus, relative to the language in which it is expressed, a truth 'grounded in meanings independently of matters of fact' (Quine 1961, p. 20). Correspondingly, an 'analytic sentence' may be defined as one expressing an analytic truth.

[2] Some-one who says *John is not as tall as John* does not contradict himself in the way he would have done by saying *John is not as tall as himself*: in the former case, we would normally suppose that *John* is referentially ambiguous, i.e. there are two different individuals involved who happen to have the same name. Referential ambiguity also arises with deictic expressions: e.g. saying *This is Luther's translation of the New Testament, and this is the American Standard Version* does not commit anyone to the proposition that one and the same text is simultaneously Luther's translation and the American Standard Version as well.

[3] Mates 1950, p. 210. The sense of 'function' here is that borrowed from mathematics, the constituent terms and the manner of their combination being regarded as the semantic variables.

[4] An expression which is not semantically endocentric is 'semantically exocentric'. Thus, for example, the English phrase *red roof* is semantically endocentric with respect to the parts *red* and *roof* if the meaning of the phrase is uniquely

On the basis of assumptions (i)–(iii) we may generalize as follows: For any language L, let 'referentially unambiguous identity sentence' (or 'I-sentence') be defined as a two-place copula sentence ('. . . is . . .') in which each place must be filled by a referentially unambiguous referring expression of L, such that the identity statement expressed asserts the referent of the first-place expression to be (or, in the case of a negative I-sentence, not to be) identical with the referent of the second place expression. Now if the statements made in L belong to a conceptual system in which the denial that X is X is self-contradictory, a subclass of I-sentences of L will be analytic sentences. Any affirmative I-sentence will be analytic which conforms to the following rule:

r': for any first-place referring expression a which has X as its referent, the second-place referring expression does not differ in meaning from a.

For the supposition that the referring expressions in the same affirmative I-sentence might have different referents but not differ in meaning is incoherent, i.e. involves supposing that either 'a is a' might be false or 'a is b' might be false even when a and b *ex hypothesi* do not differ in meaning, or both. But, given (i) and (ii), 'a is a' cannot be false, and if 'a is a' cannot be false, 'a is b' cannot be false either, since it differs from 'a is a' only in the substitution of an expression which does not differ in meaning from a, and thus, given (iii), 'a is a' and 'a is b' do not differ in meaning.

Thus at least there is a clear explication available of the notion 'synonymy of referring expressions in I-sentences': namely, the notion of the relationship between referring expressions which differ

---

determined by the meanings assigned to *red* ('ruber'), *roof* ('tectum'), and the adjective + noun combination ('y that is x'). Whereas the phrase *white elephant* is semantically exocentric if either it has no meaning determined by the meanings assigned to *white* ('albus'), *elephant* ('elephas'), and the adjective + noun combination ('y that is x'), or, as well as this meaning, has independently some other meaning ('unwanted gift'). (The question may arise as to why, in such a case, we choose not to give a semantic analysis according to which in *white elephant* the adjective *white* may mean 'unwanted' and the noun *elephant* may mean 'gift'. One answer might be that if neither *white* nor *elephant* occur with the meanings 'unwanted' and 'gift' respectively outside the one phrase *white elephant*, then the meaning 'unwanted gift' is peculiar to that phrase and cannot appropriately be considered the product of the independent meanings of *white* and *elephant*. If, on the other hand, *white* were found in other cases meaning 'unwanted' and *elephant* in others meaning 'gift', the justification for regarding *white elephant* as semantically exocentric would lapse. This is not an entirely satisfactory answer, however, for there might be reasons, even were there other cases where *white* meant 'unwanted' and *elephant* meant 'gift', for regarding *white elephant* as semantically exocentric. One such reason would be if neither *white gift* nor *unwanted elephant* meant 'unwanted gift'.)

in form but comply with r'. It follows that if L includes I-sentences, the competent speaker's knowledge of L-synonymy may be partially explicated in these terms, and we may say that knowledge of synonymy enables the competent speaker, *inter alia*, to determine which affirmative I-sentences of the form 'a is b' reduce, by substitution of synonyms, to 'a is a'.

Any language which had r' as a mandatory rule for affirmative I-sentences would be characterized by the following features:

(1) For any communication situation such that X is the referent of a, any affirmative I-sentence of L containing a can be used to make a true identity statement about X.

(2) All affirmative I-sentences of L are analytic provided the referring expressions are not devoid of reference.

It seems clear that natural languages contain I-sentences of the type 'a is a', e.g.

(3) *The highest mountain in the world is the highest mountain in the world*

but equally clear that the generalizations formulated in (1) and (2) are counterinstanced respectively in natural languages by sentences like

(4) *The highest mountain in the world is the highest mountain in the British Isles*

and (5) *The highest mountain in the world is the highest mountain in Nepal.*

We may therefore tentatively characterize natural languages as languages in which I-sentences occur but r' is not mandatory. Thus some progress has been made towards identifying the communicational skills which flow from knowledge of synonymy in the case of the speaker of a natural language.

Further progress can be made by invoking the very powerful argument offered by Mates, applicable to any semantically endocentric sentence of L which can be used to make a true-or-false statement. If we change such a sentence solely by replacing one component expression by a synonymous expression, the resultant sentence must be synonymous with the original sentence, since, by the postulate of semantic endocentricity, the meaning of the whole has not been altered. In any circumstances under which the original sentence could be used to make a true statement, the resultant sentence can likewise be used to make a true statement, and in any circumstances under which the original sentence could be used to make a false statement, the resultant sentence can likewise be used to make a false statement. Hence 'synonymous expressions may be interchanged without affecting the meaning or the truth value of the sentences in which they occur'.[1]

The more interesting question then arises whether interchange of expressions without altering the truth value of sentences in which they occur is a sufficient condition of synonymity. On this point, Mates offers another argument, which may be summarized as follows.

In the tautological identity sentence 'a is a', a may be replaced by any expression b and the statement remains true, provided 'a is b' is also true. But if the semantically endocentric sentences of L which may be used to make true-or-false statements include sentences containing a modal operator ('N'='necessarily'), a stronger guarantee is required; for 'N(a is a)' will be true but 'N(a is b)' may be false. This stronger requirement is that 'a is b' should be not merely true, but an analytic truth. But should the semantically endocentric sentences of L which may be used to make true-or-false statements also include sentences for reporting indirect discourse, beliefs etc., even this requirement is not strong enough. For since Jones may believe that 'a is a' without believing that 'a is b', the sentence 'N (Jones believes that a is a if and only if Jones believes that a is a)' may be used to make a true statement, but 'N(Jones believes that a is a if and only if Jones believes that a is b)' a false one, even where 'a is b' expresses an analytic truth. The stronger requirement in this case is that 'a is b' should be not merely a sentence expressing an analytic truth but that a and b should be synonymous.

> 'That nothing short of synonymity will guarantee interchangeability in a language of this type follows from the fact that the truth value of a sentence "Jones believes that A" depends not upon the truth value of the constituent A but upon its meaning. If A is replaced by any other expression not having the same meaning, the truth value of "Jones believes that A" *may* be changed, which implies that the truth value of "N (Jones believes that A if and only if Jones believes that A)' *will* be changed. Consequently if two sentences A and B are not synonymous, they will not be interchangeable in all sentences of our language. Similar considerations lead to the further conclusion that if any two sentence constituents x and y are not

[1] Mates 1950, p. 210.

synonymous, then they will not be interchangeable in the true sentence,

'N (Jones believes that . . . x . . . if and only if Jones believes that . . . x . . .)'.[1]

If we accept that natural languages fall within the class of languages to which Mates's argument applies, the question remains whether or not this requirement is, as Linsky[2] suggests, 'too strong'. For what Linsky calls 'paradigmatic synonym pairs' (e.g. *bachelor* and *unmarried man*) fail to pass Mates's criterion, in view of sentences like

(6) *Jones wants to know whether a bachelor is an unmarried man* and (7) *Jones wants to know whether a bachelor is a bachelor*.

Linsky's exemplification of a 'paradigmatic synonym pair' is unfortunate, since it seems clear that *bachelor* and *unmarried man* are at least not analytically synonymous.

But we do not need to rely on paradigmatic counterexamples at all, in view of the following considerations.

In the sentence frame

(8) *Jones wants to know whether a . . . is a . . .* we can fill the two blanks either by the same form (*a* and *a*) or by two different forms (*a* and *b*). Now regardless of the meanings of *a* and *b*, it is clear that the two sentences so produced can report different things that Jones wants to know. But if that is the case, then difference of form must be a sufficient condition of difference of meaning for any language which contains sentence frames like (8) and any expressions which may fill the blanks in such frames. One consequence of this for a language like English would be that no two nouns or noun phrases are synonymous.

But postulating a difference in meaning between every noun (or noun phrase) and every other noun (or noun phrase) would not be so much too drastic a way of accounting for the difference in meaning between sentences about what Jones wants to know as a very puzzling way. For it will be far from clear in many cases exactly what semantic difference could plausibly be introduced into the σ-characterizations of pairs of expressions such as to account for their noninterchangeability in frames like (8). E.g. if it happens to be true that

(9) *Jones wants to know whether a pomelo is a shaddock* but not true that

(10) *Jones wants to know whether a pomelo is a pomelo*

[1] Mates 1950, pp. 211–212.   [2] Linsky 1967, p. 55.

then presumably Jones's uncertainty is occasioned by not knowing the exact relation between the fruit and one or both of the expressions *pomelo* and *shaddock*, i.e. Jones is uncertain as to whether or not it is the same fruit which is variously called *pomelo* or *shaddock*, but not uncertain as to whether or not a pomelo is a pomelo. What at least seems clear is that postulating a difference in meaning between *pomelo* and *shaddock* is no way of explaining how it comes about that Jones's uncertainty is correctly reported by (9) but not by (10). For that is already explained by the occurrence in (9)—but not in (10)—of the two words the co-existence of which occasioned Jones's uncertainty.[1]

From this the conclusion is not, as suggested by Linsky, that Mates's criterion is too rigorous, but rather than it is based on a requirement which is simply irrelevant.

The most obvious constraint upon setting up σ-characterizations and ρ-characterizations is that we need to be able to account plausibly for differences in the truth conditions of declarative sentences. The fact that there are communication situations in which

(11) *Jones is eating an apple*

can be used to make a true statement, whereas

(12) *Jones is eating a pear*

cannot so be used, needs to be accounted for in terms of a semantic difference between (11) and (12). Here a difference in truth conditions answers to a difference in meaning, most plausibly located in the nonequiform expressions *apple* and *pear*.

The crucial question, however, in the present context is the question when it is correct to account for the identity of truth conditions of declarative sentences by postulating their synonymity.

This is a question more often dodged than answered, as e.g. by Katz and Martin in their rejection of Ziff's scepticism about the synonymity of

The tiger ate the man

and *The man was eaten by the tiger.*[2]

Ziff argued that since 'to eat a man is hardly the same as to be eaten by a tiger' and since what is said of the tiger in one sentence is accordingly not what is said of the man in the other sentence, then

---

[1] More exactly, there occurs in such cases surface structure syncretism involving underlying lexical items and their corresponding citation forms: cf. Harris 1970.
[2] Ziff 1966, p. 231.

the claim that the two sentences are synonymous comes down to nothing more than that 'one is true if and only if the other is true'. Katz and Martin concede the interdependence of truth conditions of the two sentences, but claim that 'this fact alone would not prompt us to say that the two are synonymous'.[1] Instead, however, of saying what *would* prompt them to call the two synonymous, they advance the somewhat bizarre (in the context) contention: 'Surely, the situation is the other way around; their synonymy prompts us to say that one is true if and only if the other is.' This riposte is simply irrelevant, in the first place because Ziff had not challenged the correctness of the thesis that truth values are preserved under substitution of synonymous expressions, and in the second place because that thesis cannot be advanced to settle the question whether or not two particular sentences in a particular natural language are synonymous. If *The tiger ate the man* and *The man was eaten by the tiger* are granted to be synonymous, then it follows that one is true if and only if the other is true. But what Ziff questioned was the grounds on which their synonymity should be 'granted'.

Katz and Martin are no more convincing in their attempts to deal with Ziff's sentences *Someone is a wife* and *Someone is a husband,* and *Someone was a child* and *Someone was a parent.* They assert (invoking the authority of Chomsky and Abelard) that these pairs are synonymous and argue that, considered from the point of view of logical form, the difference between the first pair 'is only one of the order of existential quantifiers. For example, using M for "is a male", F for "is a female", and W for "is married to",' then *Someone is a wife* comes out as '$(\exists x)(\exists y)(Mx.\ Fy.\ Wxy)$', whereas *Someone is a husband* comes out as '$(\exists y)(\exists x)(Mx.\ Fy.\ Wxy)$'. But this is to beg the question against Ziff by assuming that *Someone is a wife* means the same as *Someone is a wife and someone (else) is her husband,* while *Someone is a husband* means the same as *Someone is a husband and someone (else) is his wife.* (And why stop there? If all entailments count as part of the meaning of a declarative sentence, *Someone is a wife* ought also to be synonymous with *Two people got married and someone was the vicar or priest or registrar or ship's captain. . . .*)

Since transformational semantics lacks the distinction between synthetic and analytic synonymity of sentences, it is not surprising that its apologists are forced to deny the relevance of differences of analytic meaning (which are the differences Ziff's examples raise).

---

[1] Katz and Martin 1967, p. 488.

But that does not excuse the refusal to explain how synonymity of sentences is established. For even if we were to dismiss differences of analytic meaning as irrelevant, that question still remains. It not only remains, but becomes pressing in view of such concomitant assertions by Katz and Martin as that *Some triangle is equiangular* and *Some triangle is equilateral* are 'true and false together', but that this is explained by 'geometrical theory', whereas the equivalence of Ziff's sentences is to be explained by 'semantic theory'. For just what no serious theory of linguistic knowledge can take for granted is a distinction between 'truths of geometry' and 'truths of English'. One might just as well subsume the fact that wives have husbands under the heading 'truths of matrimony'.

Cases usually cited as throwing doubt on the contention that differences of meaning are invariably associated with differences in truth conditions are certain types of conjunctive device and sentential adverb. Strawson observes that 'even sentences to which the notion of truth-conditions does seem appropriate may contain expressions which certainly make a difference to their conventional meaning, but not the sort of difference that can be explained in terms of their truth-conditions. Compare the sentence 'Fortunately, Socrates is dead' with the sentence 'Unfortunately, Socrates is dead'. Compare a sentence of the form '*p* and *q*' with the corresponding sentence of the form '*p* but *q*'. It is clear that the meanings of the members of each pair of sentences differ; it is far from clear that their truth-conditions differ'.[1]

A further class of cases is invoked by Lakoff, who explicitly rejects what she describes as the usual assumption 'that two utterances are synonymous if and only if they are identical in truth value'. Instead, she proposes that 'one must consider those sentences synonymous that could be used with the same truth value, IN IDENTICAL ENVIRONMENTS'.[2] If we find that 'they cannot both be used in the same environment' we must suppose that they differ in meaning. The evidence adduced in support of this position comes mainly from the use of indefinite quantifiers in English. For example,

I wonder if Bill would lend me some money

and *I wonder if Bill would lend me any money*

are said by Lakoff to be 'traditionally . . . considered synonymous' but in fact not to be so, since the first but not the second can be followed by the explanatory sentence *Then I can buy that new Beatle*

---

[1] Strawson 1970, p. 11.   [2] Lakoff 1969, p. 610, n. 2.

record, while the second but not the first can be followed by the explanatory sentence *I already owe him a thousand dollars*. According to Lakoff 'to exchange the two explanatory sentences in these cases would create two very odd utterances. Thus I conclude that in sentences of this type, at least, there is some difference in meaning between those containing *some* and those containing *any*.'

It is clear from this example that what Lakoff means by the condition of occurrence 'in identical environments' is that in any environment in which the occurrence of *a* is not 'odd', substitution of *b* for *a* must be possible without ensuing 'oddity'. By 'oddity' she means that 'in certain situations, confusion and misunderstanding will result'. Pairs of sentences not amenable to judgments of truth-or-falsity, e.g. interrogatives, Lakoff apparently considers to have the same truth value (i.e. presumably, none), and in such cases, therefore, occurrence in identical environments becomes the essential criterion. (Curiously, Lakoff counts conditionals as 'unfalsifiable'; but this need not concern us here.)

It may first of all be observed that the formulation of Lakoff's criterion does not quite correspond to her intentions as witnessed by the examples she gives. To insist on interchangeability in identical environments is in fact too strong a condition for Lakoff's purposes, since this will exclude otherwise 'synonymous' pairs which happen to differ in the ordering of surface elements. E.g. Ziff's

The tiger ate the man

and *The man was eaten by the tiger*

cannot both take, without ensuing oddity, the addition of the co-ordinate clause *and promptly fell asleep*. But it seems doubtful whether Lakoff intends to treat such pairs as nonsynonymous *for that reason*.

If we follow the spirit rather than the letter of Lakoff's criterion, it nonetheless supports some of Ziff's cases; e.g. it seems distinctly odd to follow the first, but not the second, of the pair

Someone is a wife

and *Someone is a husband*

with the co-ordinate clause *and therefore someone must be a wife*.

However, not all of Lakoff's interpretations are entirely convincing, because she has apparently overlooked a further *some/any* contrast, which involves the use of *some* for contextually defined reference (=*certain*). Thus *Who wants some Xs?* is commonly used when the offer is quite specific (=*I have some Xs: who wants them?*)

and contrasts with the speculative *Who wants any Xs?* (=*I haven't any Xs: but I'll see if there are any available*). Similarly, in

If you eat some spinach, I'll give you ten dollars

some may be taken as indicating that it is not just eating any old spinach that will earn ten dollars, but eating some particular spinach the speaker has in mind. Lakoff, however, treats *some* here as indicating the expectation 'that the person addressed wants ten dollars' and implying that the speaker is offering a reward, as opposed to

If you eat any spinach, I'll give you ten dollars

where 'the only possible interpretation is that, for some reason, the person addressed does not want to receive ten dollars, and that this sentence is a threat'. This seems dubious. A more natural interpretation of the latter sentence would be that the speaker offers ten dollars irrespective of *what* spinach is eaten.

The point makes some difference to Lakoff's thesis about synonymy. For if we take account of this particular *some/any* distinction, then it is doubtful whether Lakoff has in fact produced any new examples of nonsynonymous declarative sentences having the same truth conditions. E.g. it may well be true that I wonder whether Bill will lend me some money (because the sum I have in mind is considerable) but not true that I wonder whether he will lend me any money (because I know he never refuses a moderate request). And so on.

We have thus far considered only incidentally the extent to which synonymy criteria must take into account variations of linguistic and situational context. If it is conceded that expressions may have different meanings in different contexts, the possibility is open that two expressions may have the same meaning in one context but not in another, and hence the necessity arises for distinguishing between 'context-free synonymy' and 'context-bound synonymy'. (By 'context-free synonymy' is to be understood here synonymy independent of context, i.e. synonymy in all contexts.) A semantic description of L may be envisaged as accommodating such a distinction by adding supplementary qualifications to relational characterizations. Thus, for example, a suitably qualified characterization of type $\rho 1$ might take the form:

$$(a=b) \text{ C}$$

where 'C' denotes the context or set of contexts for which the semantic equivalence between a and b holds.

The type of problem which arises in delimiting context-bound

I

synonymities may be shown by means of an example. Suppose a semantic description of English distinguishes at least two meanings for the noun *paper*, one of which it shares with *newspaper* and the other with *essay*.[1] Such a description encounters the problem of specifying the values of C1 and C2 for the following relational characterizations:

(*paper=newspaper*) C1

and (*paper=essay*) C2.

Any solution to this problem must presumably take into account at least the following three considerations.

(1) On some occasions when a sentence containing the word *paper* is used, the sentence is interpreted (and is intended to be interpreted) as would be a sentence identical but for the substitution of *newspaper* for *paper*; but it is so interpreted (and intended to be so interpreted) in virtue of knowledge about a particular communication situation. An example of this case would be the sentence *The costs of publishing the paper are very high* uttered by the editor of the local weekly at a Rotary club lunch.

(2) On some occasions when a sentence containing the word *paper* is used, it is doubtful whether it is to be interpreted as under the substitution *newspaper* for *paper*, or as under the substitution *essay* for *paper*, unless further information is obtainable about the relevant situation. An example of this case would be the sentence *Professor Jones is reading his paper* uttered in circumstances where the professor might conceivably be engaged in either of two activities, namely (i) addressing a learned society, or (ii) catching up on the day's news.

(3) On some occasions when a sentence containing the word *paper* is used, no such doubt arises because the rest of the sentence makes the appropriate interpretation clear. Examples of such cases would be utterance of the sentences *The paper ceased publication* and *The paper was on the mating habits of the giraffe*.

Various answers may be envisaged to the question as to how a semantic description should deal with facts such as these. It will be assumed, for purposes of the example, that the linguist is able to verify empirically under what circumstances doubt arises about the interpretation of words in particular communication situations, and this information may thus be looked upon as constituting part of the data available for the construction of a semantic description of *L*. The

---

[1] It is not essential to the example that these expressions should in fact have in English the meanings here attributed to them.

question to be considered, therefore, is the status of this evidence as warranting or not warranting the incorporation of possible features in the description.

One possibility is that facts of the kind described in (1) should be accounted for in the description by an appropriate specification of C1, e.g. to the effect that *paper* and *newspaper* are synonymous in sentences uttered by journalists. This course would be objected to by theorists who, like Katz and Fodor,[1] claim that a semantic description of natural language cannot be expected to account systematically for the ways in which variation of situation, or 'socio-physical setting' affects the interpretation of sentences. On the other hand, it would—at least in principle—be supported by theorists who, like Lyons, claim that an identification of the relevant situational context is an essential part of the establishment of instances of synonymity.

The difference between (1) and (2) seems to be that in the former case but not the latter the appropriate interpretation of *paper* is determined by features of the communication situation known to participants in that situation. The difference between (1) and (2) on the one hand and (3) on the other seems to be that in (3) alone the appropriate interpretation of *paper* is determined by the linguistic context independently of situational features of the communication situation. Here, i.e. in (3), there would presumably be agreement between followers of Katz and Fodor and followers of Lyons that a semantic description should account for the appropriate interpretation of *paper* by an indication of its contextual synonymity with *newspaper* and with *essay* in the appropriate cases. However, the arguments which might be adduced for and against these solutions require closer examination.

According to Lyons, 'once we accept that synonymy must be bound to context, it ceases to be a theoretical problem at all',[2] and in *Structural Semantics* a procedure is proposed for establishing instances of synonymity on the basis of interchangeability in a particular linguistic context (defined by a set of sentences of the language) and a particular situational context or range of contexts (e.g. 'making a purchase in a shop'). The linguist is envisaged as examining empirically how the speaker's commitment varies under

[1] Katz and Fodor 1963.
[2] Lyons 1963, § 4.46. It is not quite clear how this statement is to be taken, i.e. what theoretical problems we are invited to see as being solved by accepting that synonymity must be bound to context.

modification of sentences in certain ways, while holding the situation-type constant. This procedure is held to determine a relationship which Lyons calls 'pragmatic implication', and knowledge of synonymy is explicated as knowledge by the speaker of certain 'pragmatic implicational' connexions between the utterance of certain sentences in certain types of situation.

For the description of natural languages accessible to experimental investigation by the linguist, Lyons would propose to establish an instance of synonymity as follows:

'Let us take two utterances which differ formally in one respect only and let that difference consist in the occurrence of a form *a* in the one utterance at the point at which an item *b* occurs in the other: *We have a wide range of cigars* and *We have a wide selection of cigars*. These two utterances, we will suppose, have been heard in a tobacconist's shop, and we are interested in seeing whether the forms *range* and *selection* are synonymous here. (Our reason for thinking that they might have the same meaning could be based on a 'hunch' or even on the statement to that effect by the native English speaker.) The test whereby we establish that two complete utterances of this kind are synonymous is, in principle, behavioural and empirical.

'The first problem is to delimit the context of situation. There is no need to exaggerate the theoretical difficulties of this. . . . Let us here assume that the linguist has provisionally identified as the same situational context (itself 'culture-bound') the events and activities which constitute making a purchase in a shop. The linguist can satisfy himself that the utterances *We have a wide range of cigars* and *We have a wide selection of cigars* occur in this context, if he is thorough in his methods, by going around and exasperating several tobacconists with his 'informant-technique'. He can then try the effect of substituting different items in place of *cigars*. Assume that he has collected a number of utterances of the form *We have a wide (range/selection) of* (____); that is, a number of utterances in which *range* and *selection* are interchangeable, and therefore have meaning. . . . The question now is to decide whether the forms *range* and *selection* have the same meaning in these utterances. This does not consist simply in asking the informant; for this would be merely to invite him to invent some difference—say, for example, that the use of *selection* implies that he has chosen his stock with care. But the problems connected with testing the informant's response to the substitution of the two items in the frame, though they exist, are problems of a practical nature, as are the problems of devising tests for identifying variants in phonology. The aim is to inveigle the informant, without prejudice to the issue, into accepting or refusing to accept utterance *a* as a 'repetition' of utterance *b*. If *a* has not the same meaning as *b* it will either not imply something which *b* implies or imply something which *b* does not imply. And it should not be beyond the practical ingenuity of the linguist to discover this.'[1]

What might well be questioned in connexion with Lyons's method, however, is whether it is not beyond the practical ingenuity of the linguist to determine systematically all the types of situation in which a context-bound synonymity holds.[2] If a serious attempt were made to delimit all the situations in which *paper* and *newspaper* receive identical interpretations, it would doubtless soon become apparent that a very complex weighting of the importance of different factors in the situation operates. It is highly unlikely, for example, that a criterion as simple as 'utterance by journalists' will turn out to be correct. (If it were, then the semantic description of English would lead us to expect that an appropriate response to the eminent journalist who, about to address a learned society, announces 'I have mislaid my paper' might be 'Don't worry: there's time to go out and buy another.') Nonetheless—the theorist of context-bound synonymy might argue—the practical difficulty of the enterprise of discovering in exactly what situations two words are synonymous does not impugn the validity of the concept.

We may pursue the matter further by considering the following proposal:

(K) '*a* and *b* are context-bound synonyms in contexts of type C if and only if in contexts of type C the substitution of one for the other does not affect the commitment of the speaker.'

It is of interest to examine what the consequences of a strict application of such a criterion would be in the construction of our semantic description of *L*.

The first consequence we may note is that equivalence of illocutionary acts[3] becomes a sufficient condition of synonymity, since the criterion proposed leaves the linguist free to set up as

---

[1] Lyons 1963, § 4.46.

[2] Katz and Fodor adduce the fact that it is practically impossible to produce a systematic analysis of all conceivable ways in which variation of 'socio-physical setting' may affect the interpretation of sentences as a reason for rejecting the view that a semantic theory should take situational context into account (Katz and Fodor 1963, p. 489).

[3] On illocutionary acts, see below Ch. 5.

context-bound synonyms any two expressions for which a context-type C can be established such as to permit the substitution of expressions in certain sentences without affecting the commitment of the speaker in that context.

Thus consider the case of Picasso, who, called upon to identify a forgery, has the choice between uttering the sentences *This is not a Picasso* and *This is not a work of mine*. In this context the two sentences, and the two constituents *a Picasso* and *a work of mine*, may be regarded as context-bound synonymous expressions. It would be unavailing to object to this proposal that the commitment is different in the two cases, since in saying the former Picasso does not commit himself explicitly to the proposition that the work in his, while in saying the latter he does not commit himself explicitly to the proposition that it is by Picasso. This difference would indeed be relevant if we were being asked to consider the sentences in abstraction from the situational context; but under K what we are asked to attend to is, quite specifically, what Picasso commits himself to in that situation. In short, if pairs of sentences have illocutionary equivalence in a certain type of context, we may count the expressions which contrast as context-bound synonyms. (If we were pedantically inclined, we could of course require Picasso to identify the forgery by uttering some such formula as *I, Picasso, certify that this is not a work of mine*. But this alters nothing, since the following formula will do just as well: *I, Picasso, certify that this is not a Picasso*.)

But this has the following consequence. If in defining a situational context or range of situational contexts it is permissible to include a necessary condition Q such that Q specifies the relation of the speech acts in question to particular language-users or particular times and places, then there is no guarantee that a pair of context-bound synonyms will not include a deictic and a non-deictic member. Now any theory of synonymy which allows this may require us to concede e.g. that 'my-English' is semantically different from 'your-English', that the English spoken on the first of January is not the same language as the English spoken on the second of January, etc. The proposed criterion, in other words, permits the distinction within a 'language' of indefinitely many situationally-bound 'sub-languages', each with its own semantic rules and synonyms.

There is, it might perhaps be urged, nothing methodologically vicious about that, provided we are prepared to forego generalization.[1]

---

[1] Nonetheless, *quot homines tot linguae* seems a curious theoretical basis for linguistics.

But unfortunately there is a further consequence, namely the failure to distinguish semantic from extralinguistic knowledge. This vitiates the method even in the investigation of the most strictly delimited sublanguage. The argument in support of this criticism is simply that if the interpretation of an expression depends on certain features of the communication situation, as distinct from the expression used, then to that extent the interpretation is not a matter of semantic knowledge. Thus, to take Lyons's example, supposing the linguist's investigation is confined to the semantics of 'shopping English', or, more strictly still, to the semantics of 'tobacconist's English', even then the method proposed offers no sound basis for reaching the conclusion that e.g. *range* and *selection* are (or are not) synonymous. For it incorporates no way of distinguishing between the respects in which the speaker's commitment is based on knowledge of certain facts about the situation, and the respects in which the speaker's commitment is based on knowledge of the meanings of the words used. To know that X is a tobacconist, or a journalist, or a bank manager, or to know that a conversation is taking place in a tobacconist's shop, or a newspaper office, or a bank, is to know—so the argument would run—something about the world in which one lives, not something about the language one speaks. If the purpose of a semantic description is to account for communication by postulating semantic knowledge shared by language-users, it requires a method of investigation which distinguishes evidence of semantic knowledge from evidence of extralinguistic knowledge.

The objection that criterion K involves a failure to distinguish questions about speech acts from questions about the meanings of expressions may also be pressed on the basis of examples like the following:

Consider the sentences:

(1) *Yes*

(2) *I was in Bognor Regis on the 1st of January 1967*

(3) *I would not be telling the truth if I denied it*

The speech act of confirming my presence in Bognor Regis on the 1st of January 1967 when asked *Were you in Bognor Regis on the 1st of January 1967?* can be realized by my uttering (1), (2) or (3). But to say that this constitutes evidence of the context-bound synonymity of (1), (2) and (3) would be quite plainly to confuse two different senses of 'meaning', i.e. confusing what the words 'mean' with what someone's uttering them 'means'. The special context does not confer synonymity upon (1), (2) and (3), any more than other contexts render them nonsynonymous. What the context does is afford *me* the choice of meaning the same thing by uttering (1), (2) or (3).

The further problem of determining what a speaker is 'committed to' by uttering a sentence in a given context may be illustrated by an example given by Bennett:

(8a) *At this moment he's on a train going to London*
(8b) *At this moment he's in a train going to London.*

Setting aside, for purposes of the example, the somewhat extraordinary possibility of interpreting (8a) as meaning that he is on the roof of a train going to London, we may ask: are *on* and *in* here context-bound synonyms? But, first of all, are (8a) and (8b) synonymous in the context? Bennett is inclined to regard this as a case of 'coextensiveness' rather than synonymity: for, he argues, these sentences 'would normally describe the same situation, but it would be counter-intuitive to postulate some high-level linguistic unit that can be realized alternately as *on* and *in*, since *on*-ness and *in*-ness are essentially different notions, i.e. $on^{s\text{-}t}$ and $in^{s\text{-}t}$ differ in cognitive meaning. What we have, rather, is a case of coextensiveness. There are certain situations in reality that can be perceived by a speaker of English as involving either *on*-ness or *in*-ness. One such situation is the boarding of a train, which can be perceived as getting *onto* it or getting *into* it. Thus whether one uses *on* or *in* in (8), the situation described is the same.'[1]

Setting aside the stratificationalist trappings, what Bennett's answer comes down to is that (8a) and (8b) differ in meaning, but in such a way that the difference is always irrelevant in the context. Since stratificational theory leads him to hold that 'synonymy depends on the realizational phenomenon known as 'diversification',[2] he is inclined to reject the synonymity of (8a) and (8b) because he cannot imagine a plausible unit which could here undergo 'diversification'. This may be good stratificational theorizing, but it is not convincing linguistic analysis. For to approach the problem in this way is to assume the availability of (nonlinguistic) criteria for deciding questions of conceptual classification. The nature of these criteria is allowed to remain obscure, e.g. we are not told why '*on*-ness' and '*in*-ness' are 'essentially different notions'.[3] But worse still, the argument

---

[1] Bennett 1968, p. 164.   [2] Bennett 1968, p. 159.
[3] This is a puzzling assertion. It is not as if it would be out of the question to imagine a language which simply did not make the English distinction between *on* and *in*, but had only a single locational preposition translating both.

propounded simply assumes what needed to be demonstrated, namely that *to be on a train* and *to be in a train* here correspond to a 'genuine' conceptual difference. Precisely what is at issue is whether English recognizes a difference, not whether in the abstract a difference might conceivably be recognized.

On the other hand, the application of criterion K yields no happier solution, since it is not clear what evidence we would look for to decide whether a speaker takes on different 'commitments' in the context of describing X's whereabouts by uttering (8a) and (8b). And if this is not clear, it is because the notion of 'commitment' itself is not clear.

More remains to be said about the validity of setting up context-bound synonyms as a way of accounting for instances where a choice between interpretations is resolved by the linguistic context, independently of situational features.

Reference has already been made to the rejection by Katz and Fodor of the thesis that a semantic description should take situational variation into account. Having pointed out that the possible ways in which situational factors may affect the interpretation of sentences are virtually limitless (hence not amenable to systematization), they conclude that a semantic description is adequate if it accounts only for interpretational variations dependent on the linguistic context.

The basis of this view is that 'except for a few types of cases, discourse can be treated as a single sentence in isolation by regarding sentence boundaries as sentential connectives.'[1] Katz and Fodor argue:

'As a matter of fact this is the natural treatment. In the great majority of cases the sentence break in discourse is simply *and*-conjunction. (In others, it is *but*, *for*, *or*, and so on.) Hence, for every discourse, there is a single sentence which consists of the sequence of *n*-sentences that comprises the discourse connected by the appropriate sentential connectives and which exhibits the same semantic relations exhibited in the discourse. But since the single sentence is, *ex hypothesi*, described by a theory of semantic interpretation, in every case in which a discourse can be treated as a single sentence, a theory of semantic interpretation is as descriptively powerful as a theory of setting selection.'[2]

In support of this view, Katz and Fodor adduce the following considerations.

[1] Katz and Fodor 1963, p. 490. [2] Katz and Fodor 1963, pp. 490–491.

'To illustrate this, let us consider the two-sentence discourse: "I shot the man with a gun," "If the man had had a gun too, he would have shot me first." The first sentence of this discourse is ambiguous in isolation, but not in this setting. But the problem of explaining this disambiguation is the same as the problem of explaining why the single sentence "I shot the man with a gun, but if the man had had a gun too, he would have shot me first," does not have an ambiguous first clause. Likewise, consider the discourse, "I heard the noise," "The noise was completely inaudible," and its single sentence equivalent, "I heard the noise, and the noise was completely inaudible." In showing why the single sentence is anomalous, a theory of semantic interpretation exhibits precisely those semantic relations in which the anomaly of the discourse resides. This technique of replacing discourses or stretches of discourses with single compound sentences, by using sentential connectives in place of sentence boundaries, clearly has a very extensive application in reducing problems of setting selection to problems of semantic interpretation of sentences in isolation. Thus, given a theory of semantic interpretation, it is unclear how much is left for a theory of setting selection to explain.'[1]

Katz and Fodor concede that not all discourse can be converted straightforwardly into single sentences, but do not see this as a serious objection.

'For example, the discourse "How are you feeling to-day?" "I am fine, thanks," does not convert to "*How are you feeling to-day and I am fine, thanks" because the compound sentence is ungrammatical. But the fact that sentences of different types cannot be run together in the obvious way may not pose a serious problem because it is not at all clear that less obvious conversions will not lead to a satisfactory treatment of such cases within a theory of semantic interpretation. For example, we may convert the discourse just cited into the single sentence, "X asked, 'How are you feeling today?' and Y replied, 'I am fine, thanks'." If such conversions can be carried out generally, then any problem about disambiguation, detection of anomaly, and so on that can be raised and/or solved in a theory of setting selection can be raised and/or solved by reference to an analogon in the theory of semantic interpretation. But even if such conversions cannot be carried out generally, the most interesting

[1] Katz and Fodor 1963, p. 491, n. 12.

and general cases will still be within the range of a theory of semantic interpretation.'[1]

Thus in a semantic investigation of the kind envisaged by Katz and Fodor setting up context-bound synonyms would be one possible way of accounting for the fact that two sentences which do not receive the same semantic interpretation in isolation do so when forming part of certain longer discourses. For example,

(1) *Smith read his paper*

and (2) *Smith read his newspaper*

will be, we may assume, given different interpretations in isolation by a semantic description of English, since they have different truth conditions. But considered as first sentences in the two-sentence discourse formed by the addition of, say,

(3) *He looked first of all at the stop-press on the back page*

they receive, let us assume, identical interpretations. If Katz and Fodor's proposals are accepted, these two-sentence discourses may be treated as the compounds

(4) *Smith read his paper, and looked first of all at the stop-press on the back page*

and (5) *Smith read his newspaper, and looked first of all at the stop press on the back page.*

Accordingly, one possible way of accounting for the interpretation of (4) and (5) would be postulation of the synonymity of *paper* and *newspaper* in certain contexts, the contexts in question being defined so as to include (4) and (5).

Setting up context-bound synonymities is also a possible way—although not necessarily a theoretically desirable way—of dealing with certain other types of case. For example, the sentences

(6) *John grows flowers*

and (7) *John grows roses*

will, we may assume, be represented by a semantic description of English as having different meanings in isolation. Consider, however, the two-sentence discourses comprising (6) followed by (8) and (7) followed by (8):

(8) *Roses are the only flowers John grows.*

These two-sentence discourses can be treated as the compounds

(9) *John grows flowers, and roses are the only flowers John grows*

and (10) *John grows roses, and roses are the only flowers John grows.*

[1] Katz and Fodor 1963, p. 491, n. 12.

It is relevant to note at this point that if we follow Lyons then, given appropriate informant response, both (4) and (5) and also (9) and (10) can be established as containing context-bound synonyms. The expressions *paper* and *newspaper* will be context-bound synonyms in the frame '*Smith read his* ——, *and looked first of all at the stop-press on the back page*'; while *flower* and *rose* will be context-bound synonyms in the frame '*John grows* ——*s, and roses are the only flowers John grows.*'[1]

Now a semantic description of the type envisaged by Katz and Fodor might deal with (9) and (10) in one of three possible ways. The first possibility is that (9) and (10) are represented as semantically different (i.e. as having one or more readings not shared). The second possibility is that (9) and (10) are represented as semantically equivalent (i.e. as sharing all readings) in virtue of the fact that *flower* and *rose*, although not in isolation synonymous, are in certain contexts (of which (9) and (10) are examples) assigned the same reading. The third possibility is that (9) and (10) are represented as semantically equivalent in virtue of an operation of the relevant projection rules, whereby the difference in meaning between *flower* and *rose* is not allowed to contribute a difference in meaning to the eventual readings for the sentences (9) and (10).

An examination of these three possible solutions shows that whether to set up *flower* and *rose* as context-bound synonyms must depend on the answer to the prior question whether (9) and (10) are synthetically synonymous. If they are not, it follows that the description should not be allowed to represent *flower* and *rose* as synonymous in this context. But no way of arriving at the crucial decision is proposed by Katz and Fodor, since they do not offer external criteria for synonymity. Lyons's proposals, on the other hand, offer a solution, but manifestly the wrong one, since that would not distinguish the case of (9) and (10) from the case of (4) and (5).

---

[1] It suffices under Lyons's proposals to establish that (9) 'pragmatically implies' and is implied by (10). Pragmatic implication and pragmatic equivalence are defined in terms of 'assertion' and 'denial'. E.g. in the case of antonyms such as *single* and *married*, 'the denial of either one is implicitly equivalent to (implies and is implied by) the assertion of the other. (More precisely, the denial of a sentence containing either one, S_1, is equivalent to the assertion of a sentence, S_1^*, containing the other.). The linguist establishes this by investigating responses of informants. 'He will find, for instance, that the informant, having asserted a sentence of the form *X is single* will reject a sentence *X is married*—perhaps adding indignantly *I said once that he wasn't*, or something of the sort.' (Lyons 1963, pp. 88–89.) In the present example, the informant, having asserted either of the pair (9) or (10), is committed under pain of inconsistency to the assertion of the other.

It should be made clear at this point that the rejection of a notion of 'context-bound synonymy' which treats the two cases alike is not based on a covert argument from 'intuition'. It might perhaps be urged that it would be counterintuitive to propose a solution which treated *rose* and *flower* as synonyms in (9) and (10), but intuitively satisfactory to treat *paper* and *newspaper* as synonymous in (4) and (5). But we do not need to rely on intuitive satisfaction here, for there is a reason for distinguishing the two cases which does not appeal to intuitions at all. The pair (9) and (10), unlike the pair (4) and (5), falls under a general rule for English whereby the truth of the conjunction of a sentence 'only xs are P' and a sentence 'xs are P' stands or falls with that of a corresponding conjunction of sentences 'ys are P' and 'only xs are P', provided xs are a proper subset of ys.[1] In such cases, the postulation of a context-bound synonymity is otiose, i.e. it does not contribute to an explanation of the facts to suppose that a particular relation (context-bound synonymity) holds between two expressions, when the facts are already explained by a general rule which does not require that supposition. No such consideration applies to (4) and (5), where the postulation of a context-bound synonymity provides an explanation which cannot be derived from a corresponding general rule.

An example where criterion K leads to a postulation of synonymity which conflicts with a better linguistic explanation of the case would be:

(11) *No-one was in the room with John*
(12) *No-one was in the room except John.*

Here criterion K gives *with* and *except* as context-bound synonyms, a solution which is obviously wrong in view of such evidence as e.g. that we can have beside (12), without changing the meaning, *No-one except John was in the room*, whereas *No-one with John was in the room* is not equivalent to (11).

Further, consider the sentences

(13) *Hilary climbed Everest*

and (14) *Hilary climbed the highest mountain in the world.*

If we assume that a semantic description of English will exhibit these sentences as having different meanings in isolation, the question arises how to represent the interpretation of the two-sentence discourses comprising (13) preceded by (15), and (14) preceded by (15):

---

[1] Here xs are roses, ys are flowers and P 'grown by John'.

(15) *Everest is the highest mountain in the world.*

These two-sentence discourses can be treated in the familiar way as the compounds:

(16) *Everest is the highest mountain in the world and Hilary climbed Everest*

and (17) *Everest is the highest mountain in the world and Hilary climbed the highest mountain in the world.*

Now if a speaker is identically committed by an assertion formulated either in the way represented in (16) or in the way represented in (17), then it follows by criterion K that *Everest* in its second instantiation in (16) and *the highest mountain in the world* in its second instantiation in (17) can be treated as context-bound synonyms. This seems to be the case, since it would be inconsistent for a speaker to affirm (16) but deny (17), or vice versa.

However, it is an adequate justification of the speaker's 'commitment' in this case that *Everest* and *the highest mountain in the world* be granted to refer here to the same unique entity. In other words, the required condition is merely that there is just one x such that (i) x is called 'Everest', and (ii) x is the highest mountain in the world. Thus the 'context-bound synonymity' here assures us only of identity of reference, which is inadequate. Any theory of synonymy which allows this must be rejected, since it fails to distinguish between what is referred to by the use of an expression in a certain context or contexts, and what the expression means.

Context-bound synonymy of the kind where the context in question is situational is a notion which seems unlikely to be helpful when it comes to explaining how a speaker's knowledge of synonymities enables him to detect the analyticity of certain sentences. In such cases at least, it appears, the construction of a semantic description of L requires us to be able to set up ρ-characterizations without situational limitations.

It is not perhaps clear whether all natural languages afford the possibility of characterizing a statement as analytic,[1] but it is at least clear that many of them do. Such languages may be considered to be 'nonextensional' languages in the sense defined by Quine,[2] i.e. as possessing devices equivalent to a modal adverb 'necessarily' which yields truth when and only when applied to an analytic statement.

---

[1] It is, in any case, possible to imagine one into which one would have difficulty in translating English sentences characterizing a statement as analytic.

[2] Quine 1961, pp. 29–30.

In the sentences of such languages, interchange of expressions having identical extension does not guarantee preservation of the truth of a statement. Quine designates the stronger relation which must hold between expressions in order to preserve truth values under substitution in the sentence of nonextensional languages 'cognitive synonymy'.[1] His argument is:

'Interchangeability *salva veritate* is meaningless unless relativized to a language whose extent is specified in relevant respects. Suppose now we consider a language containing just the following materials. There is an indefinitely large stock of one-place predicates (for example, '*F*' where '*Fx*' means that *x* is a man) and many-place predicates (for example, '*G*' where '*Gxy*' means that *x* loves *y*), mostly having to do with extralogical subject matter. The rest of the language is logical. The atomic sentences consist each of a predicate followed by one or more variables '*x*', '*y*', etc.; and the complex sentences are built up of the atomic ones by truth functions ('not', 'and', 'or', etc.) and quantification. In effect such a language enjoys the benefits also of descriptions and indeed singular terms generally, these being contextually definable in known ways. Even abstract singular terms naming classes, classes of classes, etc., are contextually definable in case the assumed stock of predicates includes the two-place predicate of class membership. Such a language can be adequate to classical mathematics and indeed to scientific discourse generally, except in so far as the latter involves debatable devices such as contrary-to-fact conditionals or modal adverbs like 'necessarily.' Now a language of this type is extensional, in this sense: any two predicates which agree extensionally (that is, are true of the same objects) are interchangeable *salva veritate*.'[2]

It follows, according to Quine, that unless there is an assurance that *L* is nonextensional interchangeability *salva veritate* is too weak; for that *bachelor* and *unmarried man* are interchangeable *salva veritate* in an extensional language guarantees no more than that *All and only bachelors are unmarried men* is true. There is no assurance here that the extensional agreement of 'bachelor' and 'unmarried man' rests

---

[1] The term 'cognitive' is here intended to rule out of consideration whether the expressions in question have the same 'associations', the same 'emotive value', the same 'poetic overtones', etc., and to indicate that one is concerned simply with the use of words in expressing statements to be judged true or false, and as conforming or not conforming to the patterns of valid inference.

[2] Quine 1961, p. 30.

on meaning rather than merely on accidental matters of fact, as does the extensional agreement of 'creature with a heart' and 'creature with kidneys'.[1] However, 'if a language contains an intensional adverb 'necessarily' . . . or other particles to the same effect, then interchangeability *salva veritate* in such a language does afford a sufficient condition of cognitive synonymy.'[2]

The argument can be adapted to fit various types of expressions, including proper names and sentences. Two declarative sentences *a* and *b* in a nonextensional language are cognitively synonymous if interchangeable *salva veritate* within biconditional formulations of the type 'Necessarily, *a* if and only if *b*'.

Since we cannot assume that nonextensionality is a linguistic universal, Quine's argument leaves us asking the question: how about extensional languages? For no reason has been offered for rejecting identity of extension of predicate expressions as a sufficient condition of *L*-synonymity where *L* is an extensional language. In order to show that this possibility too must be rejected, it is relevant to divide Quine's class of extensional languages into two subclasses, which might be termed 'Extensional 1' (or 'E1') and 'Extensional 2' (or 'E2'), according to whether or not in any such language it is possible to formulate an analytic truth other than a logical truth. We should thus have a three-level hierarchy of languages. At the 'lowest' level ('E2') are languages in which logical truths are the only non-synthetic truths which can be formulated. At a 'higher' level ('E1') are languages in which logical truths and other analytic truths can be formulated but cannot be characterized as analytic. At the 'highest' level ('nonextensional') are languages in which logical truths and other analytic truths can be both formulated and also characterized as analytic (by means of such devices as the modal 'necessarily').

If now, by fiat, we remove from the English language all devices equivalent to Quine's modal 'necessarily', but make no other changes, we are left with a language which qualifies as extensional, i.e. is such that in no shape or form can we translate into it a proposition to the effect that such-and-such is necessarily true. Let us call this language 'English-E'.

Let us next consider the question whether English-E is an E1 language or an E2 language, and let us grant for the sake of the argument (a) that in the world of speakers of English-E no bachelors are married, nor are there any unmarried men who are not bachelors,

[1] Quine 1961, p. 31.   [2] Quine 1961, p. 31.

and (b) that in the world of speakers of English-E no creature with a heart is kidneyless, nor are there creatures with kidneys but without a heart.

Now to say that English-E is an E2 language will be to maintain that the statements expressed by the English-E sentences

(1) *All and only bachelors are unmarried men*

and (2) *All and only creatures with a heart are creatures with kidneys*

are either false or, if true, nonanalytic. But neither statement, *ex hypothesi*, is false: therefore both must be held to be nonanalytic.

But if both (1) and (2) are true but nonanalytic, a semantic description of English-E must include the relational characterization

($S\rho$i) '*bachelor* $\neq$ *unmarried man*'

since if *bachelor* and *unmarried man* have the same meaning in English-E, (1) states a truth guaranteed by the meanings of the words, i.e. an analytic truth. Thus for an E2 language identity of extension of expressions will not be a sufficient condition of synonymity.

However, there seems to be no reason which precludes the supposition that a semantic description of English-E could include the following relational characterizations

($S\rho$ii) '*bachelor* = *unmarried man*'

($S\rho$iii) '*heart* $\neq$ *kidney*'

(granted appropriate substantive characterizations to guarantee the internal consistency of the description).

But if $S\rho$ii is correct, the statement expressed by (1) is analytic, since its truth is guaranteed by the meaning of (1), the negation of which is self-contradictory. It follows that English-E is an E1 language, since it affords the possibility of formulating an analytic truth other than a logical truth. If $S\rho$iii is correct, then *creature with a heart* and *creature with kidneys* are, if semantically endocentric, nonsynonymous. But in that case, identity of extension does not guarantee synonymity of expressions in an E1 language, since the pairs *bachelor* and *unmarried man*, and *creature with a heart* and *creature with kidneys* are each *ex hypothesi* co-extensional pairs in English-E.

It follows that whether English-E is an E1 language or an E2 language, in neither case is identity of extension a sufficient condition of synonymity of expressions. But since English-E must be one or the other, identity of extension has been shown to be an inadequate criterion of synonymity for extensional languages.

This still leaves unanswered Quine's question about the source

K

of the assurance that the agreement between certain co-extensional terms 'rests on meaning rather than merely on accidental matters of fact'. For the descriptive linguist concerned with the analysis of natural languages, the assurance must ultimately lie in empirical tests of some kind. The problem may therefore be put in the form: what kind of test could give this kind of assurance?

Failure to deal with this question vitiates Katz's claim[1] to have solved precisely 'the problem of distinguishing analytic and synthetic truths raised by W. V. Quine'. In Katz's analysis, the characterization of a particular sentence as analytic or synthetic depends ultimately on the semantic descriptions assigned to individual words in it. But since no account is given of the method for assigning semantic descriptions to individual words, the explanatory force of Katz's 'solution' is nil.[2]

When, in a later paper,[3] Katz addresses himself specifically to the question of empirical tests for determining the analytic sentences of a natural language, he offers the following proposal:

'We present speakers with short lists of sentences. List A contains only sentences that are clear cases of what we would regard as analytic. Lists B, C, D, etc. contain clear cases of sentences that are not analytic, but, say, respectively, synthetic, contradictory, anomalous, etc. Then, we give the speakers a batch of sentences of all sorts and ask them to place these on the lists to which they belong. Each sentence is to be put on the list with whose members it is similar. If this experiment is conducted properly and if the predictions that the semantic component of the grammar makes match the actual sorting performed by the speakers (cases that are put on list A are those and only those that are predicted to be analytic, and so on), then we can claim that we have evidence, obtained in a quite unobjectionable fashion, in favour of the semantic component, as a result of its successful predictions about the data. However, the qualification that the experiment be conducted properly is extremely important. If the controls used in the experiment ensure that the members of the short lists A, B, C, etc. are sufficiently different from one another in the appropriate

---

[1] Katz 1964.
[2] It needed at least to be shown that the evidence for assigning semantic descriptions to words was independent of the assessment of sentences containing them as 'synthetic' or 'analytic': otherwise the demonstration of the distinction must be circular.
[3] Katz 1967b.

respects, then there will be no spurious common features that might lead speakers to classify sentences on the basis of irrelevant linguistic properties (e.g. in the case of list A, on the basis of some linguistic property other than analyticity). Positive results in this experiment can be interpreted to mean that the judgments of the speakers reflect a recognition of the analyticity of the sentences concerned. We can say, then, that our definition of analyticity, which enabled us to predict the outcome of the experiment, describes the concept of analyticity employed by the speakers as their implicit criterion for identifying analytic sentences, i.e. for differentiating those of the test sentences that are similar to the members on list A from those that are not similar to them. We can say this on the grounds that assuming that this is their criterion provides us with the best explanation of the behavioral data obtained in the experiment.'[1]

But this will not do either. Obviously, for any *x*, if *E* is an example of *x* we can construct informant tests designed to elicit further instances judged to be 'like *E*'. A test based on this principle, however, falls short of what is required in at least three ways. First, as Quine in his brief rejoinder to Katz points out, different lists will presumably be required for English and for e.g. French, but 'no linguistically general method is offered for making such lists'.[2] Second, even for one language the test is in principle inadequate unless there is a prior guarantee that list A contains all the possible types of analytic sentence in the language, and only those. But where does this guarantee come from? For the problem under discussion is precisely how to draw up such a list. If only what Katz calls 'clear cases' are included in the list, the test is simply a test of likeness to 'clear cases', not a test for delimiting the class of analytic sentences. Thirdly, nothing assures us that the analytic sentences of a natural language will have in common only their analyticity; consequently, Katz's test is not powerful enough to reveal what the criterion of analyticity is, but only powerful enough to elicit from informants a set of sentences judged to be 'like other (*ex hypothesi* analytic) sentences'.

Thus a 'likeness' test offers no answer relevant to the question of distinguishing analytic from synthetic; rather, it assumes that distinction already drawn. Indeed, unless it *were* already drawn, the claim that the semantic component is able to 'predict' analytic

[1] Katz 1967b, pp. 50–51.
[2] Quine 1967, p. 53.

sentences would lack substance. But as long as the method of constructing semantic characterizations for individual words remains obscure, no explanatory advance has been made. For it is there that a cleavage between semantic and extralinguistic knowledge must first be introduced if we are dealing with any kind of semantic theory which treats the meanings of sentences as functions of component variables.

We have so far discussed no consideration which requires us to revise our original proposal concerning the relationship between ρ-characterizations and σ-characterizations.

There is, however, reason to believe that very many concepts, including everyday physical-object concepts, are indeterminate in the sense covered by Waismann's term 'open texture' and Carnap's 'intensional vagueness'.[1] If this thesis is correct, it must follow that for many expressions in natural languages the enterprise of constructing a *complete* substantive semantic characterization lacks feasibility, in the sense that there is no end to the series of conceivable hypotheses which would need testing in order to establish conclusively the semantic rule governing the informant's interpretation. For any given expression investigated, the main features to be incorporated in the semantic characterization will doubtless become clear soon enough; but anyone who reflects upon the matter can easily convince himself that he would be hard put to it to elaborate the finer details of his own interpretation of words such as *house, road, chair, slow, late, red*, etc., applied to objects and events in his familiar environment.

The problem of 'open texture' and semantic indeterminacy of expressions is dealt with (rather than solved) in the conventional dictionary by the introduction of a more or less arbitrary limit to the information supplied under each entry. For example, the *Shorter Oxford English Dictionary* entry for *house* tells us that this word means 'a building for human habitation, *esp.* a dwelling-place'. The same entry also indicates various other meanings for *house*, but fails to tell us e.g. whether cottages count as houses, whether military barracks count as houses, whether caravans count as houses, whether igloos count as houses, etc. It does not tell us what to make of a sentence like *That's not a house: it's a block of flats*, nor of *That's not a house: it's a palace*.

[1] Waismann 1945, Carnap 1955.

From the viewpoint of semantic theory, it is clearly unsatisfactory to have to concede that this is the best that can be done, i.e. that it is arbitrary at what point we draw the line and say that semantic description is complete. As far as synonymy is concerned, the difficulty is particularly acute in that we have so far explained semantic equivalence of two expressions as identity of their respective semantic characterizations. But if we are now to concede that the completeness of such a characterization is arbitrarily determined in each case, or that there may be some expressions for which the characterization cannot be completed, then it would seem that, at least in such cases, we have no real account of synonymity at all.

Thus a critic might object: 'It is meaningless to say that *a* and *b* are synonymous unless *a* and *b* are expressions which are semantically determinate. But if they are expressions for which the substantive semantic characterizations are incomplete and cannot be completed, the claim that *a* and *b* are synonymous can, in principle, be neither verified nor falsified. For, conceivably, although the incomplete characterizations match so far, they might not match when complete. On the other hand, conceivably, incomplete characterizations which differ might turn out to match when complete. A claim which can be neither verified nor falsified cannot be taken seriously.' Such a critic, in effect, requires a criterion of semantic determinacy as a prerequisite to claims of synonymity.

One possible way of replying to this critic would be to invoke what may be called the 'standard meaning' argument. This argument would begin by calling attention to the fact that the alleged semantic indeterminacy of expressions does not often show up in everyday discourse, and suggesting that if this is so it is because for most purposes of everyday discourse the indeterminacy does not greatly matter. Doubtless there are cases—issuing guarantees, conforming to legal requirements, giving evidence in a court of law, etc.—when it may emerge that there is uncertainty about the exact meanings of words; but these instances are on the whole few and far between, except in such specialized areas as philological and philosophical discourse. If that is so—the argument would run—then semantic description need not bother about indeterminacy any more than the average language-user does. All that commonsense requires is that we specify for a given expression its 'standard meaning', and leave dispute about marginal cases to those who are interested in logomachy.

In support of this view, it might perhaps be urged that this is just how, as language-users, we treat questions of meaning. We do not in practice resort to counting raindrops in order to determine whether it is a storm or only a shower. We understand what is meant when someone says *There was a storm* or *There was a shower* by reference to some kind of imaginary 'standard case' of a storm or a shower. Accordingly, the 'standard meaning' of an expression may be stated simply by giving an account of the relevant 'standard case'. In short, the problem of semantic indeterminacy is created—or at least highly magnified—by the very attempt to introduce irrelevant precision into semantic descriptions.

This somewhat Platonistic view has a superficial plausibility; but it will not satisfy the 'open texture' critic on various points. For it seems dubious that meaning is normally a matter of tacit allusion to 'standard cases'. There may perhaps be an imaginary 'standard case' of the cat being on the mat, in the sense that one could describe an example where no-one would quibble about whether the cat was on the mat or not, e.g. Tibs curled up asleep right in the middle of the mat. But if I say *The cat is on the mat* when, perhaps, it has only its two front paws actually resting on the mat, I am not describing some 'degenerate version' of the 'standard case'. If my description is correct, it is because this actual case, like the 'standard case', is a perfectly good instance of a cat's being on a mat.

The 'standard meaning' argument seems to confuse two quite separate issues. There is the question whether we should all agree what to say in a particular case, and there is also the question whether a given meaning can properly be defined in terms of approximation to an uncontroversial exemplar. If someone disagrees that it is the right thing to say *The cat is on the mat* when the cat has only two front paws resting on the mat, on the ground that this is not sufficiently like the standard case of Tibs curled up, then he tacitly assumes that *The cat is on the mat* is in some sense short for a more complete description of the standard case. But this is no way to refute the 'open texture' critic: *his* point is the difficulty of determining exactly what it is everyone is agreed on *because of* the difficulty of determining what it is anyone is committed to. But insofar as anyone's commitment can be determined, then in principle everyone's can be determined.

The way round this difficulty which it is proposed to take here is to revise the notion that the relational characterization '$a=b$' stands for identity of the complete substantive characterizations of a and b

respectively. Instead, it is proposed to treat synonymy as definable by reference to criteria for the formulation of substantive characterizations, i.e. we take advantage of the fact that while it may not be possible to specify complete semantic characterizations for a and b, nonetheless it may be possible to adopt a particular way of formulating the criteria governing admission or exclusion of items with respect to substantive semantic characterizations which will enable a comparison relevant for judgments of equivalence to be made.

The proposal is to let '$a=b$' stand for item-by-item matching of substantive characterizations: we opt, in other words, for treating the correctness of '$a=b$' as depending on the same items being admissible to, or excluded from, the substantive semantic characterizations of a and b.

Having made this move, we are then at risk in claiming the synonymity of a and b, in the sense that counterevidence may be produced which will refute the claim (i.e. debar a $\rho1$ characterization) without waiting for completion of the σ-characterizations.[1]

In order to validate this move, we have now to propose some way of determining whether any given item is to be admitted to or excluded from any given semantic characterization. But if any such proposal is not to be vacuous, it must be integrated in quite specific ways into a theory of linguistic knowledge.

---

[1] The move is intuitively satisfactory, in that we do not feel that we need to know *exactly* what two expressions mean in order to be sure, in many cases, that they mean something *different*.

CHAPTER FIVE

Synonymy and linguistic knowledge

It would be idle to discuss the role of synonymity statements in grammar and semantics unless it could be shown that, in principle, it is feasible to formulate procedures which will make the construction of synonymity statements for L possible. But procedures of this kind cannot be formulated independently of the adoption of some specific concept of 'linguistic knowledge'; for we cannot, ultimately, say what will count as evidence for or against a given synonymity statement unless we are clear about where the boundary between the linguistic and the nonlinguistic lies.

A concept of linguistic knowledge may be delimited with sufficient precision for our purposes by specifying (i) how much about communication-in-L is to be regarded as explained by the linguist's descriptions, formal and semantic, of the set of items constituting the linguistic expressions of L, and (ii) what conditions must be satisfied in respect of a given expression and a given item of knowledge such that the item of knowledge counts as linguistic knowledge of that expression.

On the formal side, relevant proposals have already been put forward in previous chapters. It remains to deal with corresponding questions on the semantic side.

The most ambitious concept of 'linguistic knowledge' that could be entertained would, presumably, be one which made the whole process of successful communication-in-L a matter of the linguistic knowledge of L. But if this is too ambitious, as it certainly seems, the question arises as to where a line shall be drawn between those features of communication acts (speech acts, acts of writing) which depend on linguistic knowledge, and those which involve non-linguistic judgments of various kinds.

An important factor in this decision is the evidence from natural languages that the catgory of a speech act is not uniquely determined by the particular expressions used (as might, conceivably, be the case for some non-natural languages). Since the assignment of the correct speech act category is clearly of prime importance for effective communication between language-users, this suggests an obvious place to fix our boundary, and an obvious way to do it in terms of language description. By excluding any indication of speech act categories[1] from the characterizations of the sentences of a natural language, we place a significant limitation on the postulated contribution of linguistic knowledge to speech act interpretation.[2]

[1] This would be as a general principle; but it is easy to think of certain kinds of expression (e.g. greetings, farewells) where it would be difficult to apply this principle, and absurd to boot. The difficulty in some cases of stating the meanings of expressions independently of descriptions of the specific speech acts with which they are normally associated is well known. (It is forcefully stated in Malinowski 1923.)

[2] Other proposals can doubtless be argued for: it is not so far clear that they can be argued for convincingly. Searle suggests that if 'we can reduce all illocutionary acts to some very small number of basic illocutionary types' then we might assign to the deep structure of every sentence 'a simple representation of its illocutionary type'. He rejects, however, the possibility that 'illocutionary act rules would attach directly to elements (formatives, morphemes) generated by the syntactic component, except in a few cases such as the imperative' (Searle 1969, § 3.3). Boyd and Thorne want to go further than this, but their programme seems to be based on a misunderstanding of Austin's position, e.g. they refer to 'Austin's main point, which is that a complete account of the meaning of a sentence cannot be restricted to semantic analyses as they are usually understood and that they must be extended to include information about the kind of speech act involved in uttering the sentence—that is, its illocutionary force' (Boyd and Thorne 1969, p. 58: but see Austin 1962, p. 100). They appear to envisage an analysis in terms of two basic categories: 'statements and imperatives (the latter being subdivided into commands and demands) are the primary speech acts and all others are in a sense modifications of them. The point is that it seems that the analysis of all performatives can be produced through the addition of other features to the features STATE and IMP. For example, *insist* can be used to make what might be described as a modified statement (*I insist that he went*), a modified command (*I insist that you go*), or a modified demand (*I insist that he go*). In each case the analysis of the verb *insist* differs from that of the verb *state* or the verb *command* or the verb *demand* by possessing a feature which they do not (call it [+ EMPHATIC].)' The explanatory advantage of all this is far from clear, since it merely re-analyses what would normally be regarded (cf. *Shorter Oxford English Dictionary*, art. *insist*) as three different meanings of the verb *insist*. Furthermore, the analysis is highly questionable. (Is the difference between saying *I insist that you go* and *I command you to go* a matter of a certain emphasis added to the order? And even if it were, and were only that, can the kind of 'emphasis' involved simply be equated with the kind of 'emphasis' which marks the difference between *I insist that he went* and *I state that he went*? This seems to be simply playing with words.) But questionable or not, the new analysis adds nothing to a semantic description of sentences involving *insist*, since their semantic differences are always recognized anyway (i.e. as different 'meanings' of *insist*). Nor is this all. Such cases as *insist* can be subsumed under a general rule (i.e. one applying to various other verbs as well) that utterances of sentences with the verb in the first person singular present indicative can have—but do not invariably have—the appropriate performative force corresponding to their meaning. In other words, we can better explain *what kind of* speech act is being performed on these occasions by reference to the meaning of the verb involved than by calling it an 'emphatic statement', or an 'emphatic command', etc. (Since Austin clearly realized this, it seems a pity to invoke his authority in support of such a feeble analysis.) Finally, it is doubtful whether Boyd and Thorne have a firm grasp of the notion of a speech act at all, for they assert that 'under certain circumstances we substitute one kind of

The boundary thus set up coincides with that normally assumed in post-Austinian philosophy of language, e.g. by Strawson:

'To know the meaning (or meanings) of a sentence of a language is to be at least partially equipped to understand how any serious utterance of it by a particular speaker in a particular context is to be taken. But evidently to grasp the whole of what should be taken to be intended to be understood by such an utterance is generally something more than merely to know the meaning of the words uttered. Somewhere in between grasping the former and knowing the latter comes the ability to identify any *propositions* actually expressed in the making of the utterance. It comes in between the two, on the one hand, because sentence-meaning alone, without help from the context of utterance, will rarely reveal just at what points the general concepts which figure in a proposition are there conceived as attaching to the world; and, on the other, because knowledge merely of what proposition is expressed does not include knowledge of how its expression is to be taken, or of all it is to be taken to imply. If, then, we speak of the whole of what may properly be taken to be intended to be understood by the making of a particular utterance as the *force* of that utterance, we have the trio: force, proposition(s) expressed (if any), sentence-meaning.'[1]

It should perhaps be emphasized that propositions are not here conceived of as sentence-meanings (as they have sometimes been construed).[2] They stand on the frontiers of linguistic knowledge, and their 'frontier status' is reflected in their classification into 'synthetic' and 'analytic'. Analytically true propositions constitute the limiting case in which linguistic knowledge alone takes us furthest towards comprehending the force of an utterance. To say this is, of course, to leave untouched the task of determining which such propositions are, and to this we must return below.

---

speech act for another. For example, under some circumstances we are likely to use the question *Will you pass the salt?* rather than the command *Pass the salt* and we would be surprised if someone took it as a question and not a command'. Anyone who can say this must be confused over the difference between semantic categories (e.g. 'interrogative sentence', 'imperative sentence') and speech act categories (e.g. 'question'). There is no sense in which one kind of speech act is here being substituted for another: on the contrary, *Will you pass the salt?* and *Pass the salt* are in normal circumstances both used in speech acts to which one would assign the same category, 'request'.

[1] Strawson 1967, pp. 9–10.
[2] Staal 1966, Lemmon 1966, Garner 1970.

But first it should be noted that the proposed semantic boundary for linguistic knowledge coincides reasonably well with intuitive notions of what it is to understand the meaning of a sentence, and with plausible tests for establishing whether or not someone knows what a sentence means.

For example, let us suppose that there are two readers of Kipling's *Plain Tales from the Hills* who place different interpretations upon the first sentence 'To the wittiest woman in India I dedicate this book', solely in that reader A, unlike reader B, considers that what Kipling says in that sentence might be true or false. Now we should certainly wish to say that reader A had failed to grasp something; but his failure is a failure to grasp the force of the speech act[1] rather than a failure to understand the meaning of the sentence. If there is no respect in which A's bizarre supposition about the truth-or-falsity of what Kipling says precludes A's passing all the reasonable comprehension tests which reader B would pass as to the meanings of the words exemplified, and of the exemplified devices for combining them, then the conclusion must be reached that A and B arrive at their differing interpretations on the basis of the same semantic knowledge.

Someone might, perhaps, choose to maintain that one of the key tests is what you would say if asked whether what Kipling here says is true or false, and this is the test A fails to pass. But the motivation for setting up this test is not just weak but thoroughly obscure. For the sentence in question is not one which could never be used to make a true-or-false statement at all (Kipling might conceivably have uttered it appropriately on some other ocasion, e.g. in the course of describing the book to an interviewer on the eve of its publication, to make such a statement). Reader A's mistake, therefore, seems best described by saying that he here incorrectly assigns the speech act category 'statement', although knowing perfectly well the meaning of the sentence in question.

Assigning the correct category to a speech act is characteristically unlike assigning the correct meaning to a sentence in that there is no total to be arrived at which is the product of component parts. The judgment relates to a unit which is the whole utterance, and any mistake is a mistake about the category of the whole utterance. One might be wrong about the meaning of one particular word in a sentence, although right about the rest. Such a mistake has no

---

[1] Cf. Austin 1962, p. 33 et passim.

analogue in judging the category of a speech act. For we do not (to adapt a remark of L. J. Cohen[1]) utter one word of statement and six of something else: it is the whole utterance which constitutes the statement, not any part of it. Whereas it is typically one word or group of words which constitutes e.g. the referring expression in a sentence.

Failure to pay attention to such distinctions is a potential source of confusion in semantics. It may result (as with Katz and Fodor's explanation of 'paraphrase' discussed in the preceding chapter) in a misleading use of verbs such as *say*, *mean*, applied indiscriminately both to speech acts and to expressions uttered in speech acts, or (as with Lyons's theory of 'context-bound synonymy') in a lack of clarity concerning the role of context in determining interpretation. It may also lead to confusion over such a notion as 'semantic anomaly', which plays an important part in the semantic theory of Katz and Fodor and in the discussion of analyticity generally. For example, someone might be led to consider as semantically anomalous a sentence like—to take Austin's example[2]—*I appoint this horse consul*, where the oddity is due not to the fact that the sentence lacks a plausible 'reading',[3] but to the fact that the corresponding speech act lacks force.

Such considerations argue in favour of the proposal to let the σ-characterization of an expression *a* represent the knowledge a competent speaker of *L* may draw upon in interpreting any speech act, just insofar as that interpretation is determined by the use of *a* in the speech act in question. Thus a σ-characterization is not, as such, called upon to represent the knowledge which enables the hearer to assign the correct speech act category to an utterance. The decision to limit the content of σ-characterizations accordingly may, in the case of some non-natural languages, be otiose (e.g. for languages where all speech acts belong to the same category). Nonetheless, as regards natural languages a distinction is warranted by the radical difference in the kind of judgment called for.

On this view, linguistic knowledge does not explain e.g. understanding the difference between *Go for a walk* as a suggestion and *Go for a walk* as an order, nor the difference between *You are asking for trouble* as a warning and *You are asking for trouble* as a threat,

---

[1] Cohen 1962, p. 45.   [2] Austin 1962, p. 35.
[3] On the contrary, the sentence is semantically quite appropriate for the communicational purpose envisaged, if only there existed a social procedure which gave its utterance the required force.

unless such differences are regularly signalled by linguistic means, e.g. by systematic differences of intonation.[1] In such pairs the force of the speech act may be different, while the meaning of the expressions is the same.

The distinction is of particular importance as regards synonymy, since it may be perfectly possible to find sentences which are normally used in equivalent illocutionary acts but have different meanings (perhaps *Would you mind shutting the door?* and *Shut the door if you please*),[2] and also sentences which are normally used in nonequivalent illocutionary acts, but have the same meaning (perhaps *Primatology is the study of primates* and *Primatology is primatology*).[3]

In acceptance of the foregoing there is an implicit rejection of 'neo-Austinian' definitions of meanings in terms of speech acts, e.g. the definition of sentence meaning proposed by Alston:

'S_1 means $S_2 =_{df}$. S_1 and S_2 have the same illocutionary-act potential.'[4]

and associated accounts of synonymy, e.g.

'W_1 means $W_2 =_{df}$. W_1 and W_2 can be substituted for each other in a wide range of sentences without altering the illocutionary act potentials of those sentences.'[5]

The reason why semantic definitions of this kind do not provide an acceptable basis for an account of synonymy in natural languages is quite simply that differences in illocutionary act potential can sometimes be due to a formal difference between expressions. To take up, by way of illustration, the example cited above, it is clear that there will be illocutionary acts which can be performed by uttering *Primatology is the study of primates* but which cannot be performed by uttering *Primatology is primatology*, e.g. the illocutionary act of explaining to X (as distinct from the perlocutionary act of getting X to understand) what primatology is (granted that X does not know what primatology is: for example, supposing he has asked the question 'Can you explain to me what primatology is?'). For to say

---

[1] There will doubtless be borderline cases—these may be such—where it is not clear whether we should say there is a difference of meaning.

[2] Evidence of a difference of meaning is the fact that I may say *Yes* to the first if I am objecting, whereas if I say *Yes* to the second I am signifying readiness to comply. (Someone may say *Yes* to the interrogative sentence to indicate compliance; but if he does, this shows he is taking the utterance of that sentence as having the force of *Shut the door if you please*, or something similar, i.e. his *Yes* is not, as in the other case, the answer to a question.)

[3] The first is normally, we may assume, intended to have the force of a definition, which it is difficult to attribute to the second.

[4] Alston 1964, p. 36.   [5] Alston 1964, p. 37.

to someone, in effect, 'I gather you do not understand what primatology is, but, since you ask me, I will enlighten you by telling you
that primatology is primatology' would be somewhat like saying 'I
know the door is shut, but shut it all the same'. In these and similar
cases the speaker would be failing to 'take responsibility' (to use
Alston's phrase)[1] for his speech act in the appropriate way.

What is missed in the 'illocutionary act potential' definition is
precisely the sense of 'meaning' in which the synonymity of *a* and *b*
accounts for the correctness of the explanation '*a* is *b*'.

If we accept that a semantic description of L must be based on a
prior decision to differentiate items of knowledge into two classes
(those which count, and those which do not count, as items of
semantic knowledge about particular expressions), and if the substantive semantic characterizations contained in a semantic description of L are interpreted as statements to the effect 'S (the speaker of
L) knows that . . .', then a method of formulating the content of
semantic characterizations involves a procedure for selecting certain
items from the totality of knowledge attributable to the speaker.
Such a view incurs the obligation to demonstrate that non-question-
begging tests for classifying items of knowledge in the manner
required are, in principle, available.

To take a simple case, if we treat the semantic characterization
  '*dibatag*: long-necked antelope...'
as representing the proposition:
  'S knows that long-necked antelopes...are called *dibatags*'
the formulation of the semantic characterization implies a decision to
include certain items of knowledge relating to a certain class of
animals as part of the speaker's linguistic knowledge, and to exclude
certain others. Thus for any item of knowledge about dibatags
attributable to the speaker who knows how to use the word *dibatag*
(e.g. that they have an average gestation period of *n* days, or that they
are almost extinct) the question arises whether it forms part of the
speaker's linguistic knowledge of the expression *dibatag*. This
question is, in effect, the question of delimiting what Katz and Fodor
call the 'upper bound of a semantic theory'. Its relevance to analyticity is that according as different items are included in or excluded

from a semantic characterization, so different sentences will consequentially be exhibited as analytic.
Katz and Fodor claim:

> 'Since a complete theory of setting selection must represent
> as part of the setting of an utterance any and every feature of the
> world which speakers need to determine the preferred reading
> of that utterance and since . . . practically any item of information
> about the world is essential to some disambiguations' it follows
> that 'such a theory cannot in principle distinguish between a
> speaker's knowledge of his language and his knowledge of the
> world because, according to such a theory, part of the characterization of a *linguistic* ability is a representation of virtually all
> knowledge about the world speakers share.'[1]

As an example of a piece of nonlinguistic information Katz and
Fodor cite the fact that lions, but not children nor buses, are often
kept in cages. Knowledge of this fact, they argue, would be required
for the selection of correct readings for the following three sentences:

Should we take the lion back to the zoo?
Should we take junior back to the zoo?
Should we take the bus back to the zoo?

Thus, even if informants concurred in assigning no more than one
reading to each of the above sentences in isolation, a semantic
description of English should nonetheless—on this view—mark each
sentence as ambiguous, since the informants' interpretation is here
based upon an item of information which happens to be common
knowledge, but *not* linguistic knowledge.

In the example cited, it is clear that the decision to mark each
sentence as ambiguous means excluding certain information from the
semantic characterizations of various words, e.g. we exclude from the
semantic characterization of the word *lion* any such metalinguistic
description as '...often kept in cages...'. But the question arises:
what are the grounds for this exclusion? To argue that the exclusion
is justified because the knowledge that lions are often kept in cages is
nonlinguistic knowledge would be beside the point; since for any
given item of nonlinguistic knowledge we can easily formulate a
corresponding item of information about the use of a linguistic
expression, e.g. that *lion* denotes a class of animals . . . often kept in
cages. The question that needs to be answered is why this does not
count as part of the speaker's semantic knowledge of the word *lion*.

[1] Katz and Fodor, 1963, p. 489.

The same issue is raised in a more general form by Bolinger's query: 'where do semantic markers come from?' Bolinger points out that Katz and Fodor allow that in communication situations there are occasions where 'we achieve a disambiguation by way of something that is not a semantic marker', and asks:

> 'But why is it not a semantic marker? Where do markers like (Animal), (Physical Object), (Young), and (Female) come from if not from our knowledge of the world? What is strange about (Shoe-wearing) as a semantic marker—not as general, surely, as (Female), but general enough? The discalced branch of Carmelite monks is identified by it, and it crops up every now and then as a mark of status. . . .'[1]

To such questions, however, neither Katz and Fodor nor Bolinger are able to supply an answer. Katz and Fodor take for granted a distinction between semantic and nonlinguistic knowledge, but attempt no explication of the distinction. At least two reasons require that such an attempt be made. First, until it has, the upper bound of a semantic theory remains unfixed, i.e. we have no assurance that literally any fact act all about lions (e.g. that Nero kept them as pets) might not turn out to be part of the meaning of the word *lion*. Second, as long as the upper bound of a semantic theory remains unfixed, the problem of analyticity remains unsolved, for we shall be unable to say with certainty which the analytic sentences of *L* are. As Staal observes in connexion with another example (*Whales are mammals*), 'the semantic theory of a language does not solve this problem, but presupposes its solution. For the answer would depend on the way semantic trees are constructed. For the above illustration [mammal] may or may not be considered a semantic element of the tree for *whale*, dependent on whether this zoological information is or is not considered part of the native speaker's competence.'[2]

---

[1] Bolinger 1965, p. 568.
[2] Staal 1966, p. 79. Staal, however, wants to have it all ways at once; for he claims that Katz (Katz 1964) showed how 'a semantic theory enables us to decide which sentences of a natural language are analytic. The decision can be obtained quite mechanically with the help of formal definitions for analyticity, contradiction, etc. Here no circularity is involved, since the construction of a semantic theory does not depend on notions like analyticity. . . .' (Staal 1966, p. 68). The claim that no circularity is involved is repeated (Staal 1966, p. 72). But nothing could be more patently circular; for the construction of a semantic theory depends on deciding what to count as included in the meanings of particular words, and since the type of semantic theory advocated by Katz and Fodor has as one of its objectives to explicate the semantic contribution of individual words to the sentences in which they occur, that in turn presupposes that a decision has already been taken as to whether, e.g. the fact that whales are mammals counts as semantic knowledge. If it does, *Whales are mammals* will turn out to be analytic.

The solution which seems best to meet the requirements of empirical linguistic analysis is to count knowing the meaning of an expression as including knowing that p if and only if (i) all speakers of L know that p, and (ii) the assumption that all speakers of L know that p is required to explain their normal interpretation of some sentence or sentences of L comprising or containing the expression in question.

Where p is an item of knowledge relating to the use of an expression a, we can represent p by including an appropriate metalinguistic expression π in the semantic characterization of a:

'a: . . . π . . . .'

Then the following rule (R) will govern the formulation of the content of substantive semantic characterizations:

(R): 'For any expression a, the characterization includes a metalinguistic description π if and only if (i) the information represented by π is known to all speakers of L, and (ii) the information represented by π is utilized in the interpretation of some sentence of L.'

Thus under R, if a is the expression *lion* and π is the metalinguistic expression '. . . often kept in cages . . .', for inclusion of this expression in the characterization of a it needs to be shown (a) that all speakers of L know that *lion* is a word for kind of creature often kept in cages, and (b) that this knowledge is utilized by all speakers of L in their interpretation of some sentence of L.

Testing for (a) is, we may take it, straightforward enough. Testing for (b) can be undertaken by constructing sentences about lions in which some point of interpretation (e.g. a disambiguation of pronominal reference) is dependent on knowledge of the fact that *lion* denotes a kind of creature often kept in cages, and investigating whether speakers of L utilize this knowledge in interpreting the sentences.[1]

This proposal does not incur the objection voiced by Katz and Fodor against a theory of setting selection, that it involves as 'part of

---

[1] Katz and Fodor's example is somewhat more complex than this in that the simultaneous utilization of several items of knowledge is involved, namely: '*lion*: . . . often kept in cages . . .', '*bus*: . . . not often kept in cages . . .', '*child*: . . . not often kept in cages. . . .'.   But we can run tests for the simultaneous utilization of such knowledge with sentences such as *John could see buses and children and lions in their cages*, and determine whether *their cages* is interpreted as referring to the lions' cages, or, as is syntactically possible, to the cages of the buses and children as well. It would be essential to construct the test in such a way that no information relevant to the disambiguation (e.g. that the lions were in cages, but not the buses nor the children) was supplied by the context.

L

the characterization of a *linguistic* ability . . . a representation of virtually all knowledge about the world speakers share'. This objection is met by the satisfaction of both conditions incorporated in *R*, i.e. it is not sufficient that an item of knowledge should be shared by all speakers of *L*, but it must be shown also that this item of knowledge is utilized by all speakers in their interpretation of certain sentences of *L*. It is this latter condition which provides the justification for including the relevant information in the characterization of a linguistic ability. It might perhaps be the case in some particular instance that all items of knowledge common to speakers of *L* could be shown to be utilized by the speakers of *L* in their interpretation of sentences. But if that were so it would be an empirical fact about that linguistic community, not a consequence which must follow from the adoption of *R* in the linguistic analysis of *L*. We may conclude, then, that the application of *R* satisfactorily determines the upper bound of a semantic theory of *L*.

On the basis of *R*, we may define synthetic synonymy-in-*L* by (i) making it both a necessary and a sufficient condition for relational characterizations of type $Sp1$ that there be no metalinguistic description π such that π is excluded from the substantive semantic characterization of one but not the other of the two *L*-expressions in question, and (ii) making it both a necessary and a sufficient condition for relational characterizations of type $Sp2$ that there be a certain metalinguistic description π such that π is excluded from the substantive semantic characterization of one *L*-expression but not the other.

Similarly for analytic synonymy-in-*L* characterizations of type $A\rho1$ and $A\rho2$ will involve the same guarantees for matching pairs of meaningful elements which occur as components of two synthetically synonymous expressions.

The answer thus proposed to Quine's problem of distinguishing synonyms from expressions which merely agree extensionally runs in brief as follows. Two co-extensional expressions (e.g. *creature with a heart* and *creature with kidneys*) will be counted (synthetically) synonymous if all speakers of *L* know that they are co-extensional, and utilize this knowledge in interpreting appropriate sentences containing these expressions. They will not, however, count as analytically synonymous expressions if there are semantic differences between corresponding pairs of components (e.g. *a heart* and *kidneys*). For such pairs of expressions as afford no basis for the semantic comparison of component parts (e.g. *pomelo* and *shaddock*) a distinction between synthetic and analytic synonymity cannot be drawn. We need not be moved by objections to the effect that this solution simply elevates factual knowledge to the status of semantic knowledge on condition that it play a role in interpretation. For we may reasonably, at this point, inquire of our objector what better reason he can think of for calling knowledge 'semantic'.

Accordingly, any truth expressed in a sentence of the form 'All and only *a*s are *b*s' will be analytic on condition that substantive semantic characterizations for *a* and *b* admit and exclude the same items. This can be tested empirically, since the proposals advocated above allow us to determine, for any item of knowledge whatsoever, whether it shall be represented in the semantic characterization of any given expression.

Normally, it will not be difficult to construct for *a* and *b* exactly parallel tests to decide whether a particular item shall be included in or excluded from the substantive semantic characterization. For example, we might wish to test the hypothesis that the word *bachelor* is interpreted as applying to a man who has no wife. If that hypothesis is correct, we should expect informants to be able to identify the subject of *was refused admission* in *Peter arrived at the club with John, who also brought Peter's wife in the car, but, being a bachelor, was refused admission*; to detect an anomaly in *There were twenty trade union officials at the meeting, of whom ten were bachelors and at least twelve had brought their wives*; etc. Let us suppose that the results with these tests are positive, i.e. confirm the hypothesis. Now tests can be run with the same sentences, substituting *unmarried man* and *unmarried men* for *bachelor* and *bachelors* respectively. If these tests give the same results, we conclude that both for *bachelor* and for *unmarried man* the substantive semantic characterization must be so formulated as to include the information that the expression is interpreted as applying to a man who has no wife.

When we can elicit no further items of knowledge which appear to determine how informants interpret sentences containing *a* and sentences containing *b*, and any hypothesis confirmed (or rejected) for *a* has been correspondingly confirmed (or rejected) for *b*, we may conclude that *a* and *b* are (synthetically) synonymous. They will also be analytically synonymous to the extent that similar results can be obtained for matching pairs of meaningful components.

The proposed method allows us to take account of other than 'cognitive' differences between expressions. It allows for as many different dimensions of semantic variation as we can establish to be empirically relevant to communication-in-*L*. For example, if it is established that all speakers of *L* know that *nigger* is a derogatory term, but not *negro*, and use this knowledge in assigning an interpretation to some sentence(s) of *L*, the respective semantic characterizations for *negro* and *nigger* must reflect this difference.[1]

An account of synonymy based on *R* will be adequate for purposes of the linguistic analysis of natural languages in just this sense: that it provides an unobjectionable basis for explaining what it means to incorporate into a description of *L* a statement to the effect that two *L*-expressions have, or do not have, the same meaning, and renders any such statement amenable to verification.

Such an account, however, commits us to a concept of linguistic knowledge which goes considerably beyond the notion of the 'internalized rules' of the ideal speaker-hearer of *L*. This figment of modern linguistic theory is the fashionable myth which has replaced Saussure's mumbo-jumbo about a language existing only in the collective mind of the community. But, although ideal, he has his shortcomings; and one of them is that the question of what counts as linguistic knowledge *for him* not only cannot be answered, but cannot even be raised.

If, as has been argued here, the essential function of synonymy statements in linguistic analysis is to provide nonformal equivalences on the basis of which two or more formally distinct items may be related in an appropriate way at the level of analysis in question, the search for a validation of synonymity statements becomes the search for a criterion of synonymity. Such a criterion must always, in effect, constitute a proposal as to what communicationally relevant features of expressions are to be taken into account. The possible area of disagreement over such a criterion is determined, ultimately, by the crudeness of the dichotomy 'form vs. meaning'. In the nature of the case, any solution must lie in according due recognition to the variety of dimensions of communicational relevance, and in distinguishing carefully between them. Neither what is called 'form' nor what is called 'meaning' corresponds to any one such dimension. Where

---

[1] For an analysis of some 'noncognitive' dimensions, see Osgood, Suci and Tannenbaum 1957. Cf. also Halliday 1970 for an attempt to draw in general terms a distinction between three basic dimensions of meaning, related to the functioning of language in communication situations.

dichotomies are misleading, they must give way to polytomies.

To the extent that linguistics is based on the kind of over-simplification which loses sight of the multiple roles of utterances in communication situations, it inevitably leads up blind alleys. This is one of the penalties paid for trying to force language into too restrictive a theoretical straitjacket.

Within the context of any inquiry which treats linguistic knowledge only in terms of complex pairings of 'forms' with 'meanings', the problem of validating synonymity statements is—and must remain—insoluble. But on the basis of a more detailed analysis of communicational relevance it will become possible to state more accurately the conditions of communicational equivalence with respect to which natural languages are structured. Discussion of the kind which has been presented in the preceding chapters may be regarded as merely preliminary to an investigation which opens up the possibility of replacing 'synonymy' by a more precisely defined set of equivalences, and thus providing a more adequate conceptual framework for the analysis of natural languages.

References

ABRAHAM AND KIEFER 1966. S. Abraham and F. Kiefer *A Theory of Structural Semantics*, The Hague/Paris, 1966.

ALSTON 1964. W. P. Alston *Philosophy of Language*, Englewood Cliffs, 1964.

AUSTIN 1962. J. L. Austin *How to do things with words*, ed. J. O. Urmson, Oxford, 1962.

BACH 1964. E. Bach *An Introduction to Transformational Grammars*, New York, 1964.

BALDINGER 1970. K. Baldinger *Teoría Semántica*, Madrid, 1970.

BAZELL 1954. C. E. Bazell 'The sememe', *Litera*, Vol. 1, 1954, pp. 17–31.

BENNETT 1968. D. C. Bennett 'English prepositions: a stratificational approach', *Journal of Linguistics* Vol. 4, 1968, pp. 153–172.

BLOCH 1948. B. Bloch 'A set of postulates for phonemic analysis', *Language* XXIV, 1948, pp. 3–46.

BLOCH AND TRAGER 1942. B. Bloch and G. L. Trager *Outline of Linguistic Analysis*, Baltimore, 1942.

BLOOMFIELD 1935. L. Bloomfield *Language*, London, 1935.

BOLINGER 1965. D. Bolinger, 'The atomization of meaning', *Language* XLI, 1965, pp. 555–573.

BOYD AND THORNE 1969. J. Boyd and J. P. Thorne 'The semantics of modal verbs', *Journal of Linguistics*, Vol. 5, 1969, pp. 57–74.

CARNAP 1947. R. Carnap *Meaning and Necessity*, Chicago, 1947.

CARNAP 1955. R. Carnap 'Meaning and synonymy in natural languages', *Philosophical Studies*, Vol. 7, 1955, pp. 33–47.

CATFORD 1965. J. C. Catford *A Linguistic Theory of Translation*, Oxford, 1965.

CHOMSKY 1955. A. N. Chomsky 'Semantic considerations in grammar', *Monograph Series on Language and Linguistics* No. 8, 1955, pp. 141–158.

CHOMSKY 1957. N. Chomsky *Syntactic Structures*, 's-Gravenhage, 1957.

CHOMSKY 1962. N. Chomsky 'The logical basis of linguistic theory', *Preprints of papers for the Ninth International Congress of Linguists*, 1962.

COHEN 1962. L. J. Cohen *The Diversity of Meaning*, London, 1962.

COLLINSON 1939. W. E. Collinson 'Comparative Synonymics', *Transactions of the Philological Society*, 1939, pp. 54–77.

DUCHÁČEK 1964. O. Ducháček 'Différents types de synonymes', *Orbis* XIII No. 1, 1964, pp. 35–49.

DUCHÁČEK 1967. O. Ducháček *Précis de sémantique française*, Brno, 1967.

EBELING 1960. C. L. Ebeling *Linguistic Units*, 's-Gravenhage, 1960.

FILLMORE 1968. C. J. Fillmore 'The case for case' in *Universals in Linguistic Theory*, ed. Bach and Harms, New York, 1968.

FISCHER-JØRGENSEN 1956. E. Fischer-Jørgensen 'The commutation test and its application to phonemic analysis', *For Roman Jakobson*, The Hague, 1956, pp. 140–151.

FREGE 1892. G. Frege 'Über Sinn und Bedeutung', *Zeitschrift für Philosophie und philosophische Kritik*, Vol. 100, 1892, pp. 25–50.

GARNER 1970. R. T. Garner 'Lemmon on sentences, statements and propositions', *Analysis*, Vol. 30, 1970, pp. 83–91.

GLEASON 1966. H. A. Gleason *An Introduction to Descriptive Linguistics*, revised ed., New York, 1966.

GOODMAN 1949. N. Goodman 'On likeness of meaning', *Analysis*, Vol. 10, 1949, pp. 1–7.

GRICE 1957. H. P. Grice 'Meaning', *Philosophical Review*, Vol. 66, 1957, pp. 377–388. Reprinted in *Philosophical Logic*, ed. P. F. Strawson, Oxford, 1967, pp. 39–48.

GRICE 1968. H. P. Grice 'Utterer's meaning, sentence-meaning, and word-meaning', *Foundations of Language*, Vol. 4, 1968, pp. 225–242.

GRICE 1969. H. P. Grice 'Utterer's meaning and intentions', *Philosophical Review*, Vol. 78, 1969, pp. 147–177.

HALLIDAY 1970. M. A. K. Halliday, 'Language structure and language function' in *New Horizons in Linguistics*, ed. Lyons, London, 1970.

HARRIS 1951. Z. S. Harris *Methods in Structural Linguistics*, Chicago, 1951.

HARRIS 1954. Z. S. Harris 'Distributional structure', *Word*, Vol. 10, 1954, pp. 146–162.

HARRIS 1970. R. Harris 'Deviance and citation', *Journal of Linguistics*, Vol. 6, 1970, pp. 253–256.

HOCKETT 1958. C. F. Hockett *A Course in Modern Linguistics*, New York, 1958.

JAKOBSON AND HALLE 1956. R. Jakobson and M. Halle *Fundamentals of Language*, 's-Gravenhage, 1956.

JONES 1962. D. Jones *The Phoneme: its Nature and Use*, 2nd ed., Cambridge, 1962.

KATZ 1964. J. J. Katz 'Analyticity and contradiction in natural language' in *The Structure of Language*, ed. Fodor and Katz, Englewood Cliffs, 1964, pp. 519–543.

KATZ 1965. J. J. Katz *The Philosophy of Language*, New York, 1966.

KATZ 1967a. J. J. Katz 'Recent issues in semantic theory', *Foundations of Language*, Vol. 3, 1967, pp. 124–194.

162   REFERENCES

KATZ 1967b. J. J. Katz 'Some remarks on Quine on analyticity', *The Journal of Philosophy*, Vol. 64, 1967, pp. 36–54.

KATZ AND FODOR 1963. J. J. Katz and J. A. Fodor 'The structure of a semantic theory', *Language* XXXIX, 1963. (Page references are to the reprinting in *The Structure of Language*, ed. Fodor and Katz, Englewood Cliffs, 1964, pp. 479–518.)

KATZ AND POSTAL 1964. J. J. Katz and P. M. Postal *An Integrated Theory of Linguistic Descriptions*, Cambridge, Mass., 1964.

KATZ AND MARTIN 1967. J. J. Katz and E. Martin, Jr. 'The synonymy of actives and passives', *Philosophical Review* Vol. 76, 1967, pp.476–491.

KOHLER 1970. K. Kohler, Review of S. K. Šaumjan *Problems of Theoretical Phonology*, in *Journal of Linguistics*, Vol. 6, 1970, pp. 285–302.

LAKOFF 1969. R. Lakoff 'Some reasons why there can't be any *some-any* rule', *Language* XLV, 1969, pp. 608–615.

LANGENDOEN 1969. D. T. Langendoen *The Study of Syntax*, New York, 1969.

LEMMON 1966. E. J. Lemmon 'Sentences, statements and propositions', in *British Analytical Philosophy*, ed. Williams and Montefiore, London, 1966, pp. 87–107.

LEWIS 1944. C. I. Lewis 'The modes of meaning', *Philosophy and Phenomenological Research* IV, 1944, pp. 236–249.

LINSKY 1967. L. Linsky 'Synonymity', *Encyclopedia of Philosophy*, Vol. 8, 1967, pp. 54–57.

LYONS 1963. J. Lyons *Structural Semantics*, Oxford, 1963.

LYONS 1968. J. Lyons *Introduction to Theoretical Linguistics*, Cambridge, 1968.

MALINOWSKI 1923. B. Malinowski 'The problem of meaning in primitive languages', in C. K. Ogden and I. A. Richards *The Meaning of Meaning*, London, 1923, Supplement I.

MATES 1950. B. Mates 'Synonymity', *University of California Publications in Philosophy* XXV, 1950, pp. 201–226.

McCAWLEY 1968. J. D. McCawley 'The role of semantics in a grammar' in *Universals in Linguistic Theory*, ed. Bach and Harms, New York, 1968, pp. 124–169.

MOORE 1970. T. Moore 'Synonymy and case grammar': paper read to the Linguistics Association of Great Britain, April 1970.

NAESS 1953. A. Naess *Interpretation and Preciseness*, Oslo, 1953.

NIDA 1949. E. A. Nida *Morphology*, 2nd ed., Ann Arbor, 1949.

OSGOOD, SUCI AND TANNENBAUM 1957. C. E. Osgood, G. J. Suci and P. H. Tannenbaum *The Measurement of Meaning*, Urbana, 1957.

PIKE 1947. K. L. Pike 'Grammatical prerequisites to phonemic analysis', *Word*, Vol. 3, 1947, pp. 155–172.

POSTAL 1968. P. M. Postal *Aspects of Phonological Theory*, New York, 1968.

QUINE 1943. W. V. O. Quine 'Notes on existence and necessity', *The Journal of Philosophy*, Vol. 40, 1943, pp. 113–127.

QUINE 1961. W. V. O. Quine 'Two dogmas of empiricism' in W. V. O. Quine *From a logical point of view*, 2nd ed., Cambridge, Mass., 1961.

QUINE 1967. W. V. O. Quine 'On a suggestion of Katz', *The Journal of Philosophy*, Vol. 64, 1967, pp. 52–54.

ROSETTI 1963. A. Rosetti 'Son-type et phonème', *Linguistics*, Vol. 1, 1963, pp. 58–59.

SEARLE 1958. J. R. Searle 'Proper names', *Mind* LXVII, 1958, pp. 166–173.

SEARLE 1969. J. R. Searle *Speech Acts*, Cambridge, 1969.

SØRENSEN 1963. H. S. Sørensen *The Meaning of Proper Names*, Copenhagen, 1963.

SOUTHWORTH 1967. F. C. Southworth 'A model of semantic structure', *Language* XLIII, 1967, pp. 342–361.

SPARCK JONES 1964. K. Sparck Jones *Synonymy and Semantic Classification*, Cambridge, 1964.

STAAL 1966. J. F. Staal 'Analyticity', *Foundations of Language*, Vol. 2, 1966, pp. 67–93.

STRAWSON 1964. P. F. Strawson 'Intention and convention in speech acts', *Philosophical Review*, Vol. 73, 1964, pp. 439-460. Reprinted in *Symposium on J. L. Austin*, ed. K. T. Fann, London, 1969, pp. 380–400.

STRAWSON 1967. P. F. Strawson *Philosophical Logic*, ed. Strawson, Oxford, 1967, 'Introduction', pp. 1–6.

STRAWSON 1970. P. F. Strawson *Meaning and Truth*, Oxford, 1970.

TRUBETZKOY 1939. N. S. Trubetzkoy *Grundzüge der Phonologie*, Prague, 1939. (Page references are to the 4th ed., Gottingen, 1967.)

TUGENDHAT 1970. E. Tugendhat 'The meaning of 'Bedeutung' in Frege', *Analysis*, Vol. 30, 1970, pp. 177–189.

TWADDELL 1935. W. F. Twaddell *On defining the phoneme*, Language Monograph XVI, Baltimore, 1935.

WAISMANN 1945. F. Waismann 'Verifiability', *Proceedings of the Aristotelian Society*, Supp. Vol. 19, 1945, pp. 119–150.

WEINREICH 1963. U. Weinreich 'On the semantic structure of language', in *Universals of Language*, ed. J. H. Greenberg, Cambridge, Mass., 1963.

WEINREICH 1966. U. Weinreich 'Explorations in semantic theory' in *Current Trends in Linguistics*, ed. Sebeok, Vol. 3, The Hague, 1966, pp. 395–477.

WHITE 1958. A. R. White 'Synonymous expressions', *The Philosophical Quarterly*, Vol. 8, 1958, pp. 193–207.

WINTER 1964. W. Winter 'Form and meaning in morphological analysis', *Linguistics*, Vol. 3, 1964, pp. 5–18.

WITTGENSTEIN 1958. L. Wittgenstein *Philosophische Untersuchungen*, 2nd ed., tr. G. E. M. Anscombe, Oxford, 1958.

ZIFF 1960. P. Ziff *Semantic Analysis*, Ithaca N.Y., 1960.

ZIFF 1966. P. Ziff 'The nonsynonymy of active and passive sentences', *Philosophical Review* Vol. 75, 1966, pp. 226–232.

Index

phonetic-semantic resemblance, 54, 64, 70–73
pragmatic equivalence, 134
pragmatic implication, 126, 134
proper names, 112, 113, 138

quantification of synonymy, 2, 3

reference, 112, 136
referential ambiguity, 114
referring expressions, 113–115, 150
representative function, 38, 47

semantic anomaly, 86, 107, 132, 150, 157
semantically based morphology, 54ff.
semantically based phonology, 21ff.
semantic categorization, 3, 4
semantic characterization, 102–107, 112, 113, 142, 143, 145, 152, 153, 155–158
analytic characterization, 103–105, 156
relational semantic characterization, 103–107, 111–113, 119, 123, 124, 136, 139, 142, 144, 145, 156
substantive semantic characterization, 103–105, 113, 118, 119, 139, 142, 144, 145, 150, 152, 155–157
synthetic characterization, 103–105, 156
semantic classification, 3
semantic endocentricity, 114–117, 139
semantic exocentricity, 114, 115
semantic indeterminacy, 142–144
semantic subtraction, 69

sentoid, 85–87
speech act (see also 'illocutionary act'), 108, 109, 112, 128, 129, 146–152
surface structure, 96, 97, 122
symmetric predicates, 89, 90
synonymists, 1, 3, 14
synonymity criterion, 22–25, 28–34
synonymity hypothesis, 2
synonymity statement, 1, 2, 52–54, 72, 87, 89, 96, 146, 158, 159
synonymy, 1 et passim
absolute synonymy, 23
analytic synonymy, 90–94, 118, 120, 156, 157
cognitive synonymy, 137, 138
context-bound synonymy, 123–137
context-free synonymy, 123
full synonymy, 3, 86, 87, 99
grammatical synonymy, 57
immediate synonymy, 3
intellectual synonymy, 37–39
intrinsic synonymy, 87–91, 96
perfect synonymy, 3
structural synonymy, 87–92
synthetic synonymy, 85–87, 92–94, 96, 120, 134, 156, 157
synonymy postulate, 1, 19, 21, 50

tautology, 114, 117
transformation, 87, 88, 96, 97
translation, 13, 16
truth, 112–121, 123, 133, 136
analytic truth, 114, 117, 138–140, 148, 157
logical truth, 138, 139
type (vs. token), 23, 25–30, 32, 33, 45

usage, 45–47, 50, 52, 53